OTHER BOOKS OF INTEREST

BP454 Windows 98 assistant
BP455 Windows 98 hard disc and file management
BP456 Windows 98 explained
BP457 Windows 98 applets explained
BP458 Tune up Windows 98
BP466 Understanding Windows 98 Registry

Windows 98 communications

by
Jim Gatenby

BERNARD BABANI (publishing) LTD
THE GRAMPIANS
SHEPHERDS BUSH ROAD
LONDON W6 7NF
ENGLAND

PLEASE NOTE

Although every care has been taken with the production of this book to ensure that any projects, designs, modifications and/or programs, etc., contained herewith, operate in a correct and safe manner and also that any components specified are normally available in Great Britain, the Publishers and Author do not accept responsibility in any way for the failure (including fault in design) of any project, design, modification or program to work correctly or to cause damage to any equipment that it may be connected to or used in conjunction with, or in respect of any other damage or injury that may be so caused, nor do the Publishers accept responsibility in any way for the failure to obtain specified components.

Notice is also given that if equipment that is still under warranty is modified in any way or used or connected with home-built equipment then that warranty may be void.

© 1999 BERNARD BABANI (publishing) LTD

First Published - April 1999

British Library Cataloguing in Publication Data:

A catalogue record for this book is available from the British Library

ISBN 0 85934 459 2

Cover Design by Gregor Arthur
Cover illustration by Adam Willis
Printed and bound in Great Britain by Cox & Wyman Ltd, Reading

PREFACE

The act of connecting a small computer to the phone lines to form a network with other machines has created a communications phenomenon. Now known as the Internet, the impact on the lives of ordinary people has been likened to the Industrial Revolution. The computer and modem have extended the scope of the telephone lines to transmit and receive not just speech but a variety of media - graphics, music, live video and data files as well as text in the same format as Internet pages containing active links to Web sites.

We can now send a message as an e-mail and know that it will arrive almost immediately, without the frustration of endless telephone calls to numbers which may be engaged or unattended. People around the world can use video conferencing to discuss social, business or educational matters with most of the facilities of a physical meeting. The necessity to travel along congested roads to work or to meetings is diminishing. You could, for example, live in the Lake District and send your latest manuscript, reports or designs down the phone lines to London or New York.

Windows 98 provides a host of free software to turn you PC into a complete communications system. This book is intended to give the ordinary user an overview of this communications software and how to get it up and running in the home or small business.

Much of this book may also be of interest to Windows 95 users and to the general reader wishing to become conversant with this essential new technology.

ABOUT THIS BOOK

A modem enables your computer to act as a versatile communications system. The first chapter in this book discusses the choice of fast new voice modems and how to install them. This should be useful if you don't yet have a modem or you need to fit a new model to benefit from the latest in Internet communications. However, if your modem is already up and running and you don't want to dabble in the intricacies of modems, you may prefer to omit the first chapter.

The rest of the book is devoted to communications software, most of which is provided free with Windows 98 and Internet Explorer. Some of the software components may already be set up on the Internet Explorer menu as shown right, but if not it's simply a case of installing from the Windows 98 CD.

E-mail is one of the most popular uses of the Internet and Windows 98 includes a very capable e-mail program, Outlook Express. Early chapters cover its setting up and use while an overview of the popular alternative program, Eudora Pro, is also given.

If your computer has one of the latest modems, it can act as a complete voice messaging and answerphone system offering choices from a touch tone menu. This is demonstrated using SuperVoice, the software which is supplied in the package with many new modems.

Later chapters describe conversing over the Internet using Microsoft NetMeeting for video conferencing and Microsoft Chat for socialising or serious discussion. The Windows 98 CD includes free fax software, but this is not widely publicised. The final chapter explains how to locate, set up and use this software, Microsoft Fax, to send faxes direct from Windows 98 applications.

ABOUT THE AUTHOR

Jim Gatenby trained as a Chartered Mechanical Engineer and initially worked at Rolls-Royce Ltd using mainframe computers in the analysis of gas turbine performance. He obtained a Master of Philosophy degree in Mathematical Education by research at Loughborough University of Technology and has taught mathematics and computing to 'A' Level since 1972. His most recent posts have included Head of Computer Studies and IT Manager. During this time he has written several books in the field of educational computing and was involved in the pilot studies on the first wide area networks in education, before the arrival of the Internet.

TRADEMARKS

Microsoft, MSDOS, MSN, Windows, Outlook and Hotmail are registered trademarks or trademarks of Microsoft Corporation. CompuServe is a registered trademark of CompuServe Incorporated. Netscape Navigator is a trademark of Netscape Communications Corporation. AOL is a registered trademark of America Online, Inc. Eudora Pro, Eudora Light, Web-Mail and PureVoice are registered trademarks or trademarks of Qualcomm Incorporated. QuickTime is a trademark of Apple Computer, Inc. Pace 56 Voice and Pace 56 Solo are trademarks or registered trademarks of PMC Consumer Electronics Ltd. BT is a trademark of British Telecommunications Plc. VeriSign is a trademark of VeriSign, Inc. SuperVoice and PICFAX are registered trademarks of Pacific Image Communications, Inc. All other brand and product names used in the book are recognised as trademarks, or registered trademarks, of their respective companies.

CONTENTS

1. FACTS ABOUT MODEMS 1
  Choosing a Modem 2
  The External Modem 3
  The Internal Modem 4
  Installing a Modem 4
  Testing Your New Modem 10
  Troubleshooting 13
  Flash Upgrades 18
  The ISDN Alternative 20
  Summary: Facts About Modems 22

2. E-MAIL AND THE INTERNET 23
  Introduction 23
  Connections to the Internet 25
  E-mail Programs 29
  E-mail Addresses 30
  Free E-mail Accounts 31
  Getting Online 32
  Dial-Up Networking 39
  Summary: E-mail and the Internet 42

3. OUTLOOK EXPRESS BASICS 43
  Introduction 43
  Installing Outlook Express 44
  Using Outlook Express 48
  HTML Formatting 49
  Inserting Hyperlinks to Web Pages 49
  Responding to Mail 51
  Summary: Outlook Express Basics 54

4. OUTLOOK EXPRESS FEATURES 55
  The Address Book 55
  The Inbox Assistant 57
  E-mail Attachments 58
  Sending Attachments 59
  Outlook Express Stationery 62
  E-mail Security 64
  Newsgroups and Outlook Express 66
  Summary: Outlook Express Features 68

5. EUDORA PRO **69**
Installing Eudora Pro 70
Sending an E-mail 73
Receiving New Mail 74
Troubleshooting 76
QUALCOMM PureVoice 80
Summary: Eudora Pro 82

6. VOICE MAIL **83**
Voice Software 84
Transmitting Voice Messages 85
Incoming Messages 88
Managing the System 91
SuperVoice Setup 93
Summary: Voice Mail 98

7. VIDEO CONFERENCING WITH NETMEETING .. 99
Installing Microsoft NetMeeting 101
Starting a NetMeeting Session 105
The Whiteboard 111
NetMeeting Chat 112
Sharing Applications 113
Summary: Video Conferencing with NetMeeting. 114

8. MICROSOFT CHAT **115**
Introduction 115
Installing Microsoft Chat 117
Using Microsoft Chat 118
Cartoon Characters 119
Summary: Microsoft Chat 128

9. MICROSOFT FAX **129**
Fax Software 130
Installing Microsoft Fax 131
Sending Faxes 133
Faxing from a Windows Application 136
Receiving Faxes 140
Faxing with SuperVoice 143
Summary: Microsoft Fax 146

INDEX 147

1. FACTS ABOUT MODEMS

A modem is the vital link connecting your computer to the telephone network and onwards to the World Wide Web. This chapter discusses some of the features of the latest modems and then describes fitting a modem to a computer. Windows 98 makes this task much easier than previously and the work really can be carried out by anyone. However, this chapter is, of necessity, more complex than the rest of the book. So if your computer already has one of the latest modems up and running and you don't want to delve into modem technology at this stage, just skip to the next chapter.

With the latest modems, communications can involve much more than the transfer of plain text between computers. Apart from transmitting complex graphics, fax and sound, sophisticated telephone messaging systems and video conferencing are now possible between two computers equipped with modems. ISDN is a much faster but more expensive alternative to the modem, discussed later in this chapter.

Even if you already have a modem fitted, it may be one of the slower models and lacking in performance compared with the latest "56K" type. You may wish to consider replacing it as described later in this chapter.

To make the most of these powerful new communications devices you really need a computer running Windows 98 with at least the following specification:

- Pentium Processor of at least 133 MHz
- 16 MB RAM
- 10 Megabytes of free Hard Disc space
- Plug and Play BIOS
- Spare ISA slot (for an internal modem)

or:

- Spare COM port (for an external modem)

Choosing a Modem

One of the most important factors when choosing a modem is the speed of operation. Clearly, the faster the modem, the less time required to surf the Internet or to download large graphics files to your computer. For a given communications activity, with a faster modem your connection charges will obviously be lower.

The speed of a modem is normally measured in Kilobits per second (Kbps). (A bit is a binary digit (0 or 1) and 8 bits are used to represent a character such as a letter of the alphabet). Currently the "56K" modem is gaining popularity over its slower predecessors which evolved over recent years with successive speeds of 14.4, 28.8, 33.6 K. (1 "K" being approximately 1000 bits).

56K is a *nominal* data transfer rate - the actual rate may be less due to the telephone lines being busy and technical limitations. With the new 56K modems, *uploading* (or sending) from your computer is currently limited to 33.6K while *downloading* (or receiving) may achieve speeds closer to 56K.

At the moment there are two competing standards for the 56K modem; the x2 technology from US Robotics and K56flex from the Rockwell group. Initially these two standards were incompatible, but a recent agreement has resulted in the V.90 standard. This resolves the conflict between x2 and K56flex.

56K modems can often be upgraded to the V.90 standard by downloading a *Flash Upgrade* from the Internet site of the modem manufacturer. This process is described in detail later, but briefly consists of replacing the modem's operating software, which is stored in a special bank of memory inside the modem. This "flash" memory can be overwritten with new program instructions whenever an upgrade is available.

When choosing a modem you should consider the functions you will need; the latest voice modems have sophisticated answerphone and messaging facilities, in addition to fax and Internet access. You can also use a small microphone to enable complete hands-free voice communication, removing the need for a telephone handset. One small modem can therefore streamline your desktop by replacing several bulky devices.

Full duplex modems allow communication (voice or data) between two computers in both directions simultaneously. The earlier *half duplex* systems could only communicate in one direction at a time. Full duplex modems therefore permit more natural conversations when used for voice communications.

Modems (together with a suitable camera) can be used for *video conferencing* and can distinguish between different types of incoming communication - data, fax and voice. Some modems can function independently when the computer is switched off - allowing faxes and voice mail to be dealt with at all times.

The External Modem

An external modem sits on your desktop and requires a plug for its own power supply lead. A disadvantage of the external modem is that it adds to the clutter on your desk. Fitting an external modem is easy, you simply plug it into the outside of the computer without the need to remove the metal casing. Most new computers are provided with two *serial* or *communication* ports - designated as COM1 and COM2. The ports have connectors at the back of the computer into which you plug the cables for peripheral devices like the mouse, and an external modem.

COM1 is often used to attach the mouse through a 9 pin connector. COM2 is located adjacent to COM1 and is frequently used with a 25 pin connector for an external modem.

The external modem has an array of indicator lights which report on the current activities - whether the modem is switched on, if it is sending or receiving data, fax or voice mail, etc. The external modem is portable - it can easily be unplugged and transferred to another computer.

The Internal Modem

This takes the form of an expansion card which fits inside of the computer. To fit an internal modem you therefore need a spare ISA slot inside the machine and to be happy to remove the casing of your computer and press the card into place. Since the internal modem has fewer cables, etc., it is usually cheaper than the equivalent external device

The internal modem is tidier than the external model and shielded from accidental damage. Although it's not portable like the external modem, it doesn't add to the birds nest of cables at the back of the machine. Some internal modems have a bank of small DIP switches which you must set to configure the COM port. Internal modems contain their own COM port and this is often configured as COM4.

Installing a Modem

The task of fitting a modem is not difficult nowadays and really can be carried out by anyone. Even the internal modem only requires you to undo a few screws to release the casing and then plug the modem card into a vacant ISA expansion slot. Fitting the external modem is even easier - you only have to connect a few cables between the modem and the back of the computer. If you are replacing an old internal modem with a new external one you need to remember to take out the old modem first. Then remove the software for the old modem using **Remove** in the **Device Manager** (discussed later).

The modem manufacturers usually provide adequate instructions and it is virtually impossible to fit any of the cables the wrong way around.

Windows 98 has been designed for *Plug and Play* installation. This means that newly fitted devices such as modems can be detected as soon as the machine re-starts and Windows 98 takes command. In my recent experience of setting up several internal and external modems using Windows 98, Plug and Play has taken care of the entire setup process and it has not been necessary to get involved in the technicalities of COM ports, etc. However, these topics are covered in some detail later in this chapter, in case you are unfortunate enough to encounter problems.

When you re-start the computer after installing a new modem, a message should be displayed stating that new hardware has been found and Windows 98 is installing the necessary software.

Installation of the device thereafter becomes automatic - you may at most be asked to insert one of the manufacturer's installation discs if Windows 98 doesn't have the necessary "driver" programs from within its own resources. The **Control Panel** is an essential Windows 98 tool for setting up and managing the devices such as modems, connected to your computer.

Using the Control Panel

To invoke the **Control Panel** first select **Start**, then **Settings** and click on **Control Panel**.

Two of the most useful **Control Panel** applets in the context of this chapter are **Modems** and **System**.

5

You can check that the modem has been correctly installed by clicking **System**, then selecting the **Device Manager** tab in **System Properties**. You should see **Modem** listed and clicking this reveals your particular modem, in this example the **Pace 56 Voice Modem**.

If you now highlight your modem in the list of devices and select **Properties**, the **General Tab** should confirm that the modem is working correctly.

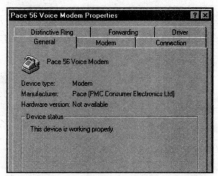

The manufacturer of your modem may also provide some diagnostic software on a floppy disc, to check that the modem has been installed correctly.

Plug but No Play

If your computer fails to detect the modem, it may be because the modem or the computer itself is not Plug and Play compatible. In this case you must use Windows 98 to detect and install the modem manually. This is done using the **Add New Hardware** applet, found in the **Control Panel**, from **Start** and **Settings**.

This invokes the **Add New Hardware Wizard** which will examine your machine for new devices.

If new devices are found you will be prompted to insert the software to enable the modem to work. This may be contained on a floppy disc or CD provided by the modem manufacturer.

Alternatively suitable software may be available on your Windows 98 CD.

The **New Hardware Wizard** should guide you through the installation of the software until the modem is finally up and running.

The Modems Applet

Another way to install a modem which has not been detected by Windows 98 Plug and Play is by using the **Modems** applet in the **Control Panel**.

Clicking on **Modems** leads to the **Modems Properties** dialogue box from where you can select **Add** to install a new modem.

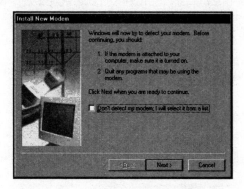

This will search for a new modem and then guide you through the process of installing the necessary software.

Once your modem is set up you can then install the communication software packages which came with the new modem, such as fax and voice messaging. With Windows 98 you already have Internet Explorer to browse the Internet; alternatively you may choose to install another browser such as Netscape Navigator.

If you are new to the Internet, you may also need to install software to connect you to an Internet Service Provider (ISP) such as the Microsoft Network (MSN) or America Online (AOL). This software may be included in the package with your new modem; alternatively it's often given away on the CDs on the front of magazines. These usually include a number of hours free Internet access time.

Testing Your New Modem

If you've previously between connected to an Internet Service Provider such as The Microsoft Network or America Online then you can try to connect to them using your previous connection number. If you have not yet signed up with an ISP, then there are other ways you can check out the dialling capability of your modem.

Phone Dialer

This is a Windows 98 accessory located in **Start**, **Programs**, **Accessories**, **Communications**.

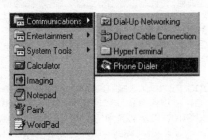

If **Phone Dialer** does not appear in the **Communications** menu shown above, then it can easily be installed from your original Windows 98 CD. From the **Control Panel** (described earlier in this chapter), select **Add/Remove Programs** then choose the **Windows Setup** tab. Now select **Communications** and **Details**. Make sure that **Phone Dialer** is ticked.

(Although Windows 98 uses the spelling "Dialer" in its menus, the general text of this book uses "dialler" and "dialling" except when referring directly to menu items.)

Click **OK** to install the new Windows 98 component, in this case **Phone Dialer**.

Phone Dialer is invoked from **Start**, **Programs**, **Accessories** and **Communications**.

If you enter a telephone number, as shown above, then click **Dial,** you should hear the modem dialling the number.

HyperTerminal

HyperTerminal is another Windows 98 accessory and resides in **Accessories/Communications** alongside of **Phone Dialer**, as shown previously. If **HyperTerminal** does not appear on the **Communications** menu, it should be installed using Windows Setup in the manner just described for Phone Dialer.

HyperTerminal is a complete communications program and is used to connect to other computers. It can also be used to test your new modem.

HyperTerminal is started by clicking on **Hypertrm.exe**

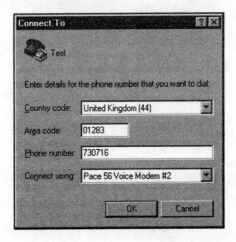

A blank window appears into which you can type various AT commands which are used to control modems. If you type **AT** and then press **Enter** you should see **OK** displayed, indicating that the COM port and modem are functioning correctly.

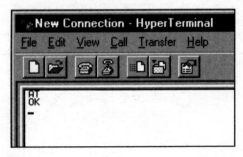

Troubleshooting

If the modem has failed to dial, you should check all of the cabling according to the manufacturer's instructions. If there's a fault in the cabling between the computer and the telephone network, there will be no dialling tone when you try to connect. You will probably see an error message similar to the following:

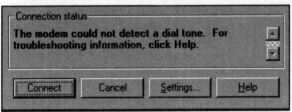

To check out the integrity of the cabling, attach a telephone handset to the telephone socket in the modem (if possible). You should hear a dialling tone and be able to manually dial up a telephone number, perhaps the connection number of an Internet Service Provider if you are already a subscriber.

Alternatively, with an external modem, the problem may be the COM port to which the modem 25 way connector is attached. Although there may be a physical 25 way connector on the rear of the computer, the ribbon cable from the back of this inside of the computer may not be plugged into the connector marked COM2 on the motherboard. (The motherboard is the main circuit board inside of the computer). This would result in an error message such as:

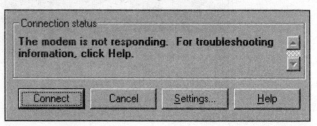

If you feel confident to remove the metal case of the computer you should be able to see the small ribbon cable connected to COM2 on the motherboard, next to the cable for the mouse attached to COM1. If the cable for COM2 is not in place, then connect it, making sure the coloured stripe on its edge is in the correct position. (Copy the orientation of the mouse cable on COM1).

If you are still unable to dial with the modem, clicking **Help** from the **Connection status** window will open up the Windows 98 step-by-step troubleshooter. This should lead towards a solution.

As stated previously, Plug and Play really does work with Windows 98 and modern computers and modems. However, if there are any problems they are often caused by conflicts between different devices trying to share the same resources. A common cause of conflict is the *Interrupt Request* setting of the communication port used for the modem, usually COM2 or COM4. These are discussed in the next section.

Interrupt Settings

An interrupt is a request from a peripheral device (like a modem) to the processor, asking the processor to give it some attention. Each device - modem, sound card, printer, mouse, etc., has a line along which it can send an interrupt request (IRQ). Each IRQ line is assigned a number in the range 0-15 (either by Windows 98 during the Plug and Play installation or manually by the user).

The IRQ number is used by the processor to decide which request to deal with next. Consequently no two devices which are likely to be used simultaneously can have the same IRQ. This applies, for example, to devices such as a mouse and a modem. These conflicts are a common cause of newly installed devices failing to work.

You can check the IRQ numbers allocated to your devices (including the modem) using **Start**, **Settings**, **Control Panel, System** and **Device Manager**. Highlight **Computer** and select **Properties**.

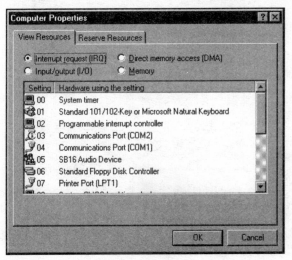

An exclamation mark against one of the devices indicates a problem in the interrupt settings.

You can see that on my machine, the port COM2 (to which an external modem is connected) has an interrupt setting of 03. No other device uses 03 so there should be no conflict.

Some modems require the IRQ numbers to be set by manually altering the "jumpers" or links which connect pairs of pins on a circuit board.

Rather than carrying out a physical modification, it may be possible to change the interrupt settings through sofware using Windows 98. First select the appropriate port (**Communications Port (COM2)** in this case) in the Windows 98 **Device Manager** mentioned previously.

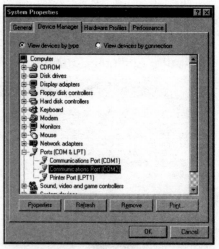

Now select **Properties** and **Resources** to reveal the settings for the port. If necessary it may be possible to alter the interrupt settings using **Change Setting...** or by experimenting with different settings for the **Basic configuration** in **Settings based on:**

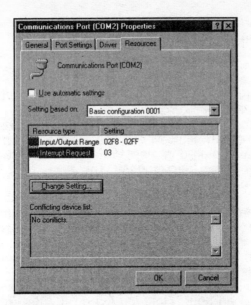

Internal modems have their own on-board communications port and this is usually configured as COM4. If necessary, you can alter the interrupt setting for COM4 after selecting **Change Setting...** in the **Resources** tab as described previously for COM2.

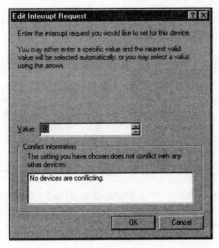

Flash Upgrades

Many of the developments in modem technology can be implemented by a software upgrade, i.e. changes to the built-in programs which control the modem. Traditionally this would involve replacing certain chips in the modem. However, a flash upgrade changes the instructions stored in a special area of battery-powered memory within the modem. The flash upgrades can usually be downloaded from the Internet.

For example, a flash upgrade is available to upgrade a Pace Voice modem from the 56Kflex standard to the newer V.90 standard. Before carrying out the V.90 upgrade you should check that your Internet Service Provider is using this standard. The flash upgrade process is quite simple and the whole job can take less than half an hour. First you log on to the Web site of your modem manufacturer. (The URL should be given in the modem documentation). For example, since I am using a Pace modem the appropriate site is:

http://www.pacecom.co.uk

Then you start the process by clicking the download button as shown below.

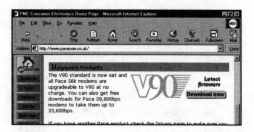

You will be asked to select the type of modem. The download only takes a few minutes, after which the upgrade program icon appears on the desktop.

Starting this enables you to unzip the program and start the **V.90 Update Wizard**.

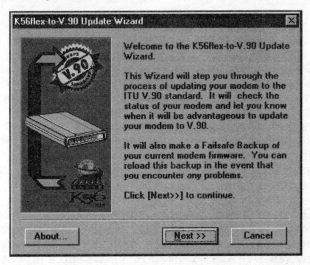

You are guided through the upgrade process with simple instructions and there is a fail safe procedure which allows you to revert to the original specification of modem if necessary. The whole flash upgrade process takes about half an hour or less and is straight forward.

A modem which is flash upgradeable is "future proof" to some extent. As new developments in modem technology evolve, some of them can be implemented by a flash upgrade to the modem software.

Checking the Speed of Your Modem

You can check the speed of your modem (*bytes received* and *bytes transmitted*) using the **System Monitor** (**Start**, **Programs**, **Accessories**, **System Tools**). This may need to be installed using the **Control Panel** applet **Add/Remove Programs** and the **Windows Setup** tab as described earlier.

The ISDN Alternative

As stated previously, the purpose of a modem is to convert binary digits coming out of the computer into analogue or sound signals for transmission along the telephone lines and vice versa when receiving data into the computer. This translation activity requires error checking and correction operations. The whole process is therefore slower than one in which the communication lines are able to handle data in digital form. Even with the fastest modems, demanding activities such as downloading very large data files from the Internet or video conferencing may be very time consuming.

ISDN (Integrated Services Digital Network) is one solution in the quest for higher speeds when transferring data, voice and video data across networks. ISDN is already in widespread use in businesses where large volumes of data and graphic files must be conveyed quickly and accurately. Until recently, the high cost of the equipment and running costs put ISDN out of reach for the home or small business user. Now, with schemes such as BT Home Highway, ISDN is becoming more affordable. The higher cost of ISDN relative to the modem is mitigated by the fact that communications activities are executed much faster, with a consequent reduction in connection charges.

There are two standards which relate to the speed of an ISDN network:

- Basic rate ISDN operating at up to 64 Kbps

- Primary rate ISDN operating at up to 1.920 Mbps.

The basic rate ISDN service is aimed at the home and small business user while larger organisations use the primary rate. It's possible to combine two 64 Kbps basic rate lines to give comunication speeds of 128 Kbps, much greater than possible with the fastest modem.

Basic rate ISDN works by utilising your existing telephone cable link to the local telephone exchange. There may be problems, for example, if the cable is an older type made of aluminium rather than copper. (The higher speed primary rate ISDN used by large businesses employs optical fibres). Some telephone exchanges are not yet supporting ISDN. Therefore it's worth checking with your telephone company before spending any money to upgrade your system to ISDN. Also check that your Internet Service Provider is geared up to provide an ISDN service.

To connect to an ISDN network your computer must be fitted with either an ISDN Card (instead of an internal modem) or a Terminal Adapter (instead of an external modem). These can now be purchased for roughly similar prices to a modem.

A common problem in many homes is the single telephone line. If someone is reading their e-mail, surfing the net or sending a fax from the computer, the line can't be used for ordinary telephone calls. The BT Home Highway ISDN 2e scheme not only solves this problem but also provides the digital communication required by ISDN.

The original analogue phone line is converted into two lines which can each use digital or analogue data. The lines can be used in various combinations: one can be used as a conventional phone or fax line while the other acts as a 64K ISDN line. Alternatively you can integrate both digital lines to give an ISDN speed of 128K. Or both lines can be used for analogue phone or fax activities. A small amount of work by a BT engineer is required to install Home Highway.

Summary: Facts About Modems

- A modem is a device for converting between the digital data used by computers and the analogue data traditionally conveyed by telephone cables.

- The latest modems conform to a standard known as V.90 and handle data at speeds up to a maximum of 56 Kbps. Flash upgradeable modems can be modified by downloading software from the Internet.

- Modems now support sophisticated voice-mail, messaging and video conferencing, apart from e-mail, fax and accessing the Internet.

- The external modem is easy to install and is portable while the internal version is neater and cheaper.

- Windows 98 offers Plug and Play, a system which greatly simplifies the installation of devices like modems. Both the modem and the computer must be of modern design and Plug and Play compatible.

- Modems are connected to the computer through devices known as communication or serial ports. External modems frequently use COM2 while the internal version often connects to COM4.

- Problems occur when the modem conflicts with another device already installed, by trying to use the same interrupt setting (IRQ).

- ISDN is a faster but more expensive alternative to the modem. Working entirely with digital data, it is the preferred choice of large businesses. Most domestic telephone lines can be modified to use ISDN. The cost of converting to ISDN has fallen considerably in recent years.

2. E-MAIL AND THE INTERNET

Introduction

This chapter looks at the principles of e-mail and the setting up of an e-mail Internet connection. This connection can be used for other methods of Internet communication such as newsgroups, chat, video and audio conferencing as discussed later in this book.

E-mail involves the sending of messages electronically between computers anywhere in the world. Mail on its outward journey from your computer is handled by an SMTP server (Simple Mail Transfer Protocol) belonging to your Internet Service Provider. Then the messages are delivered to the "POP3" (Post Office Protocol) mail server of your recipient's Internet Service Provider. The POP3 server is a computer which stores the *incoming* messages until the recipient downloads the mail to their machine. (An IMAP server is an alternative to the POP3 type and allows the user to manage incoming mail on the server itself, rather than downloading everything to the PC on their desk.)

With e-mail you don't have to make direct contact with the other person - who may be away from their computer or otherwise engaged. If the recipient happens to be online they can read the new mail immediately. Otherwise the new mail waits on the server until the next time the recipient logs on to the Internet to read the mail.

A major advantage of e-mail over conventional post is the ability to send multiple copies to a wide distribution list. You simply select the recipients' names from an electronic *address book* which you have previously created with your e-mail program. E-mails can be sent showing the circulation list of every recipient or they can be sent "blind" - so that a recipient doesn't know who else has seen the message. Other advantages include the ability to send an immediate reply and to forward a message on to someone else.

E-mails can be printed on paper or saved as files on your hard disc and archived in folders, making management of the mail neat and efficient.

Apart from speed, e-mail is much tidier than conventional mail using paper, stamps and envelopes. Longer documents should be entered into your e-mail program "off-line", to save Internet connection charges. Many e-mail programs such as Outlook Express and Eudora, allow text to be formatted in HTML like a Web page, with different fonts, graphics and links to Web sites embedded in the text.

You can also append various files from your hard disc, so that the e-mail itself consists only of a short covering note. These files, known as *attachments,* would typically consist of lengthy Word or Excel documents, video clips, digital photographs or computer programs. I have used e-mail to "post" large Word files containing text and graphics (similar to the chapters in this book), when urgently needed by the printers.

If you are sending e-mail which is personal or confidential there are options to *encrypt* the text to make it meaningless to all but the intended recipients, who possess a key to decode the message.

On the negative side you may be bombarded with unwanted advertising and junk mail (known as "spam") or with hoax e-mails intended to spread alarm. Or, because of its convenience as a rapid and reliable form of communication, your work may generate a daunting volume of e-mails which you personally need to read and reply to every day - taking valuable time away from more creative or productive activities.

E-mail Requirements

The Windows 98 CD provides all of the software tools needed to set up your machine to start sending and receiving e-mails. There are also alternatives from companies other than Microsoft, which some people prefer to use.

Since e-mail is an integral part of the Internet, getting connected to the Net is the first priority. At one time this was quite complex but now with Windows 98 and its Internet Connection Wizard the task is quite easy.

A PC capable of running Windows 98 is the basic requirement, with a modem correctly set up and connected to a telephone line, as described previously in this book. In order to send and receive electronic mail, you also need:

- A Connection to the Internet provided by an Internet Service Provider (ISP) or an Online Service.

- An E-mail Program

- An E-mail Address

Connections to the Internet

In order to use the Internet (for both e-mail and browsing the World Wide Web), you need to open an *account* with a company providing Internet access. This should enable you to connect to the Internet via one of their server computers, using a telephone number which they provide. Typically you pay for their services by a monthly or yearly subscription, although recently there has been a spate of "free" connection services. These must be judged in the context of the quality of the services and support available.

To avoid receiving horrendous telephone bills, connection to the Internet must be available at the *local* telephone rate.

When you start to set up a connection to the Internet using Microsoft's Internet Connection Wizard, you are presented with a choice of companies. These fall into two categories, **Online Services** and **Internet Service Providers**. The **Online Services** are provided by companies such as America Online, CompuServe and The Microsoft Network (MSN). Some of these were in existence before the Internet really took off and contain their own closed news and information pages which are only accessible to their subscribing members.

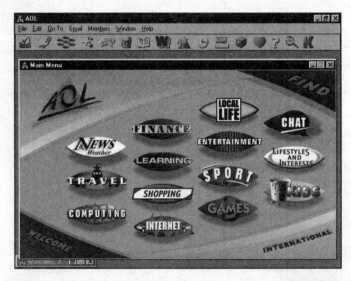

You can see some of these companies by double clicking on the Online Services folder on the Windows 98 desktop.

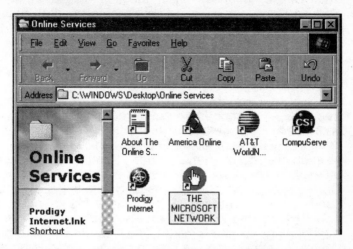

The **Internet Service Providers (ISPs)** offer a specialist connection service to the Web, without the private news and information pages produced by the Online Services.

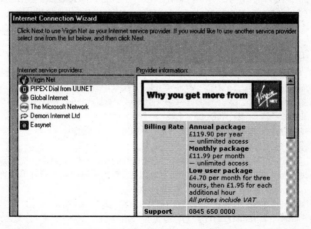

Since their business is more concerned with connecting you to the Web rather than providing information *content*, the specialist ISPs should theoretically be faster and cheaper than the Online Services.

The Online Services also function as Information Service Providers (ISPs). Therefore, in general, future references to ISPs in this book should be taken to include the Online Services. (The Microsoft Network appears in the previous lists for the two types of service.)

Many of the Internet Service Providers offer a 30 day free evaluation period but you will normally have to give your credit card details at the outset. You can often obtain CDs containing trial Internet connection software free on the front of magazines. Some of the larger players in the field such as America Online (AOL), CompuServe and The Microsoft Network (MSN) may send you a CD in the post, if you have found your way onto their mailing list. You can also start the ball rolling by opening up the Online Services folder on your Windows 98 desktop (as shown on the previous page) and double clicking on one of the icons.

Signing up for an Internet account is incredibly easy, but you have to give your credit card details before the trial period begins, so you're virtually committed from the start. You must therefore be able to cancel the account at the end of the trial period - if you're not satisfied with the service you've experienced. The onus is on you to stop the subscription - otherwise your monthly payments will start automatically. It's a good idea to find out and carefully note the arrangements (telephone number, etc.) for cancelling the account before committing your hard earned cash.

At the time of writing a number of companies are offering a "free" Internet connection service (not just for a limited trial period of 30 or 100 hours).These include Dixons and PC World whose Freeserve CD can be collected from any of their stores. It's early days to assess the quality of these services but as with all of the Information Service Providers careful comparisons of quality of service should be made.

Some criteria for choosing an Internet Service Provider or Online Service might be:

- Speed and reliability when connecting to the Internet.

- Telephone access numbers available at *local* telephone rates, in different geographical locations.

- The monthly or yearly subscription charges.

- The number of e-mail addresses per account.

- The provision of a good telephone support service.

- Support for the latest technology (such as 56K V90 modems)

- In the case of Online Services, the usefulness of the members-only information pages provided.

E-mail Programs

All of the services provide e-mail facilities and the Online Services have their own built-in program. With the other Internet Service Providers you will probably use a stand-alone program (or e-mail "client") such as Eudora Pro or Eudora Light.

The main functions of the software are to handle the sending and receiving of e-mails and any attached files. They also provide a system for the management and archiving of messages and the creation of an electronic address book. Popular packages such as Microsoft Outlook Express and Eudora Pro are discussed in the next chapter.

E-mail Addresses

When you sign up for an Internet account you will be able to choose, or be given, your own e-mail address. This is a unique location enabling your mail to reach you from anywhere in the world.

Common types of e-mail address are as follows:

stella@aol.com

james@msn.com

enquiries@wildlife.org.uk

The part of the address in front of the @ sign is normally your *user* name or Internet *login* name. The second part of the address identifies the company or organisation. The last part of the address is the type of organisation providing the service.

In the previous addresses **.com** refers to a commercial company, but other organisation types include:

.edu   education
.gov   U.S. government
.org   non-profit making organisations
.co   UK commercial company

Finally the e-mail address may end with a two digit code to denote the country, such as **uk** or **fr**. An exception to the above format is the CompuServe system of addressing which uses numbers instead of letters to identify the person, for example:

101345.2577@Compuserve.com

CompuServe have also introduced a modified system, in which the numbers can be replaced by a name.

Free E-mail Accounts

Some Internet providers only allow you to have one e-mail address unless you open and pay for further accounts. However, there may be a time when you need more than one e-mail address, perhaps for different members of your family or to separate business and social correspondence. A number of companies offer free e-mail accounts - the only obvious drawback being that you may have to endure additional advertising. One of the well-known free e-mail services is Hotmail, operated by Microsoft and sponsored by advertising. This service is intended for people who are already paying for one e-mail account through their subscription to an Internet Service Provider or Online Service.

It is extremely easy to set up a new Hotmail account - just fill in a few personal details after logging on to the Web site at:

www.hotmail.com

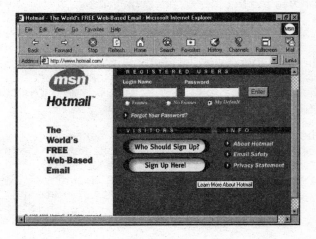

Hotmail is based on a World Wide Web site and uses your Internet browser rather than specialist e-mail software. Web-based e-mail provides easy access from remote locations anywhere in the world. You can also use Hotmail to read the e-mail you have received through your conventional e-mail accounts with other services. Since Hotmail is based on the Web, it is possible to include links to Web sites in your e-mails.

Getting Online

This section assumes your computer has Windows 98 installed and the modem is up and running. It is also assumed that you have set up an Internet browser such as Microsoft Internet Explorer. There are several ways to launch the process of connecting to an Internet Service Provider or Online Service. Many of the services provide a free CD which just needs putting in the drive then following the instructions on the screen. Or you can open up the **Online Services** folder on the Windows 98 desktop and start the process by double clicking on the service of your choice. Alternatively you can use the Internet Connection Wizard.

Whichever method you use you will need to enter the same basic information. Much of the process involves no more than filling in personal details such as name, address, telephone and credit card numbers and clicking the **Next** button. You will also need to choose a login name and password.

The Internet Connection Wizard simplifies what used to be quite a troublesome process. There should be an icon **Connect to the Internet** on the left of the desktop. Double clicking this will launch the **Internet Connection Wizard** to guide you through the process of getting online.

Alternatively you can start the wizard from **Start**, **Programs**, **Internet Explorer** and **Connection Wizard**.

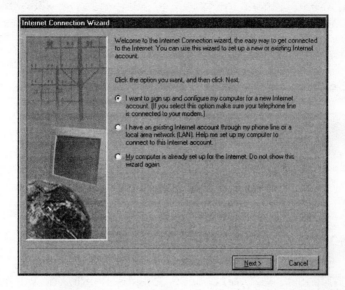

Assuming you are setting up a new account, you will now be connected to the Microsoft Referral Service which presents you with a list of the available Internet Service Providers in your area.

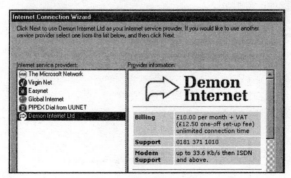

This gives details not only of the monthly charges for the service but also any additional facilities provided. Most important is the telephone number which can be used to cancel the account, if necessary, after the expiry of any free trial period.

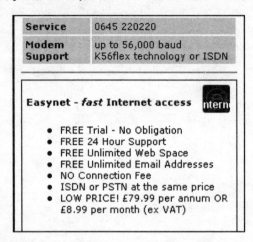

Whichever ISP you choose to subscribe to you will be presented with dialogue boxes which require you to enter your personal details such as name, address, telephone number and the details of your credit card. If you are subscribing to America Online you are advised to have the necessary information ready beforehand.

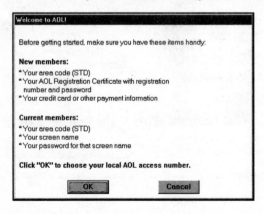

If you choose to subscribe to the Microsoft Network you will be asked to finish with the Internet Connection Wizard and start the MSN set up from its icon on the desktop. You are informed of progress at each stage.

When signing up for a new account with MSN (and other ISPs) you are asked to provide full details of your name, address, telephone number and credit card. Then you enter a user name and password.

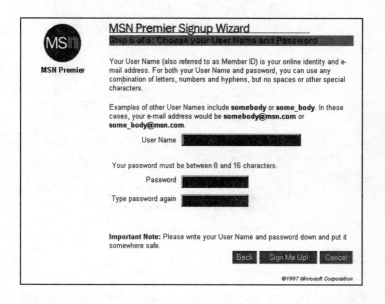

Before accepting a new login name the system checks to see if anyone else is already using it.

Whichever service provider you choose, you will need to set up a telephone number to dial into at your ISP. This must give calls at the *local rate*.

MSN provides a **Phone Book...** containing the available numbers.

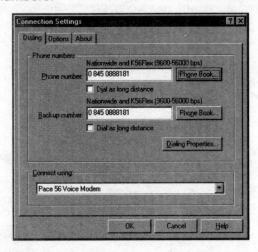

AOL chooses a number for you to dial into based on the area code that you have supplied during the AOL setup process.

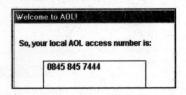

It's a good idea to check with your telephone company (such as BT) that your Internet connections really will be charged at the local dialling rate.

If you're using a BT phone line for your Internet connection, make sure your Internet dialling number is included in your list of frequently-used numbers attracting discounts under the BT Friends and Family scheme.

MSN requests you to enter your **User name** and **Password** and these can be "remembered" by ticking a box.

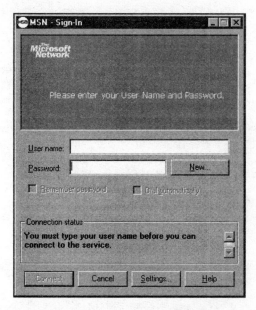

At the end of the MSN set up process any new versions of the software are downloaded automatically.

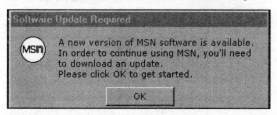

This completes the main tasks in setting up an Internet connection. If subscribing to an Online Service such as MSN or AOL your e-mail program should now be ready to use. Stand-alone e-mail programs like Eudora Pro require further setting up, covered later in this book.

E-mail Settings

The use of wizards in the set up process shields the user from many of the obscure technicalities of the e-mail system. However, you may need to examine some of the settings later and posssibly modify them. Important settings include the names of the mail servers, your e-mail address, and the telephone number which is used to dial up your e-mail service.

If you are using MSN and Outlook Express, you can examine the mail servers off-line by first double clicking the icon for Outlook Express. (To work off-line in Outlook Express click **Cancel** if it shows the MSN sign-in box). Now click **Tools**, **Accounts...**, **MSN Mail**, **Properties** and **Servers**. You can make changes to the names if necessary but you should note the original settings first.

As you can see from the previous **MSN Mail Properties**, POP3 (Post Office Protocol) is the server type for incoming mail and this is a general standard. The outgoing mail is dealt with by an SMTP (Simple Mail Transfer Protocol) server.

The **General** tab includes the name of the mail account and your e-mail address.

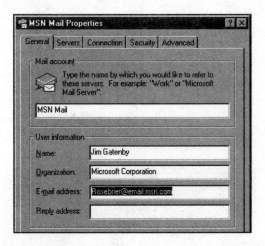

Dial-Up Networking

This is a Windows 98 component which allows you to connect to other computers including the servers of your Internet Service Provider. The dial-up connection will normally be created seamlessly during the Internet set up process previously outlined. However, the Dial-Up Networking feature enables you to examine and modify existing connections and to create new ones.

You can examine the dial-up connection settings by double clicking **My Computer** on the Windows 98 desktop and then double clicking **Dial-Up Networking**.

Dial-Up
Networking

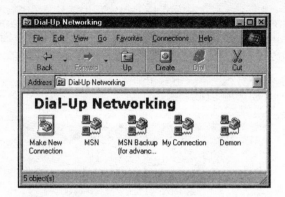

To examine the Demon connection, for example, click the right button over its icon and select **Properties**. This is where you might change the number which is used to dial your Internet Service Provider.

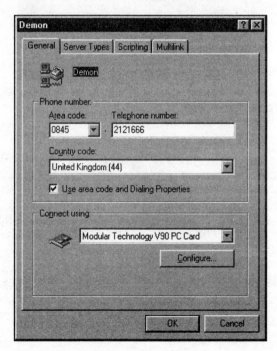

Note that apart from the area code and dial-up telephone number, Windows 98 has detected the modem type. There are numerous further settings to configure your modem, accessible by clicking the **Configure…** button. I have always found the default settings to work satisfactorily.

You can set up a new dial-up connection manually after double clicking the **Make New Connection** icon in the **Dial-Up Networking** folder in **My Computer**.

Make New Connection

First you give a name to the connection - such as the name of the Internet Service Provider. Then you enter the telephone number you wish to dial up.

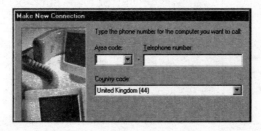

After you click **Next** and **Finish** an icon for this new connection is added to your Dial-Up Networking folder. You can dial-up your ISP by double clicking on the icon you have just created.

To enable Internet Explorer to use your new dial-up connection right click over the Internet Explorer icon then select **Properties**, **Connection**, **Settings…** and click the connection you want from the drop down list in **Use the following Dial-Up Networking connection:**.

To enable Outlook Express to use the new dial-up connection select **Tools**, **Accounts…**, **MSN Mail** (or your own account name), **Properties**, **Connection** then select from the drop down list in **Use the following Dial-Up Networking connection:**.

Summary: E-mail and The Internet

- E-mail involves the sending of text messages electronically around the world.

- Messages are normally plain text, but you can also include HTML formats with links to Web sites, graphics and various types of file as attachments.

- Incoming mail goes to a "POP3" mail server where it waits to be downloaded to the recipient's machine.

- To send e-mail, you need to subscribe to an Internet Service Provider or Online Service such as America Online (AOL) or The Microsoft Network (MSN).

- Software is available which gives free connection to the Internet for a limited evaluation period, after which it must be paid for. Some companies offer an unlimited free connection service.

- Criteria for selecting an ISP include speed of connecting, support and extra services provided.

- Windows 98 uses Dial-Up Networking to provide the telephone connections to other computers such as the servers of your Internet Service Provider.

- The number used to dial your Internet Service Provider must be charged at the *local* rate.

- Recipients of e-mail are identified by a unique address of the type: **james@msn.com**. Additional addresses may be obtained from free e-mail services such as Hotmail run by Microsoft.

- Sending and receiving messages is managed using special e-mail software such as Microsoft Outlook Express and Eudora Pro.

3. OUTLOOK EXPRESS BASICS

Introduction

Outlook Express is Microsoft's own e-mail program and is a component of Windows 98 and the Internet Explorer. If you've already established a connection to the Internet using the Internet Connection Wizard and The Microsoft Network, then Outlook Express should have been set up seamlessly, as part of the process.

You can, however, use Outlook Express as a stand-alone e-mail "client" with a connection service other than The Microsoft Network, such as Virgin or Demon Internet. Conversely, users of Microsoft Windows 98 and Internet Explorer are not compelled to use Outlook Express - you may choose a package such as Eudora Pro as discussed in the next section.

However, Outlook Express has many powerful features for the sending, receiving and management of electronic mail and is easy to set up and use - it's also free on your Windows 98 CD. There are many advanced features including encryption to increase the security of mail and the embedding of HTML Web formatting and hyperlinks in e-mail body text.

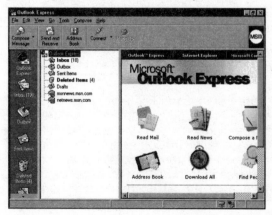

Installing Outlook Express

As mentioned previously, Outlook Express is a component of Windows 98 and is usually set up automatically as part of the installation of Internet Explorer. However, if for any reason the program needs installing on your machine, select **Start**, **Settings**, **Control Panel**, **Add/Remove Programs** and the **Windows Setup** tab and make sure **Microsoft Outlook Express** is ticked.

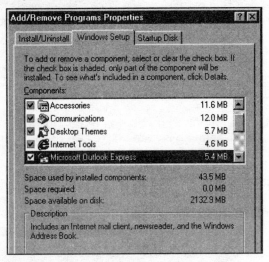

Setting Up a New E-mail Account

If you are using The Microsoft Network, then the setup procedure is greatly simplified by the MSN wizard which does virtually everything for you. If however, you are using one of the other Internet Service Providers you will need to enter the details of your e-mail account. This information should be to hand before you start to set up a new e-mail account using Outlook Express. The details should be provided by, (or agreed with) your Information Service Provider, when you sign up, as described in the previous chapter. They will probably confirm the details by traditional letter post shortly after you sign up electronically. However, total accuracy is required, so if there's any doubt it's worth contacting the ISP support desk by telephone, then noting down the details and keeping them in a safe place. Errors in this information are a common cause of problems with e-mail and Internet connections. You will need to enter:

Your Name

When sending an e-mail, your own name as you would like it to appear.

Internet E-mail Address

The address which people use to send you an e-mail. For example:

stella@msn.com

E-mail Server Names

The names of the computers used by your Internet Service Provider to handle the mail. For example:

Incoming mail server: pop3.demon.co.uk
Outgoing mail server: post.demon.co.uk

Internet Mail Logon

The login name and password which you have arranged with your Internet Service Provider.

Friendly name

A name you give to this particular account, as it will appear in the list accessed from **Tools**, **Accounts...** shown on the next page.

To create a new e-mail account, launch the program by double clicking on its icon on the desktop or from **Start**, **Programs**, **Internet Explorer** and **Outlook Express**.

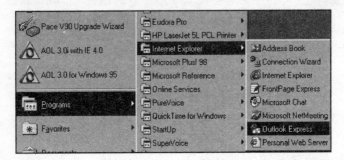

Now select **Tools** and **Accounts...**. You will see a window listing all of the accounts already set up.

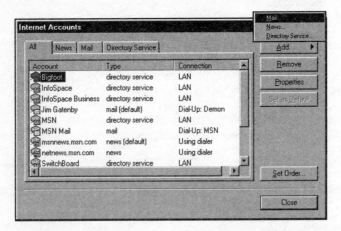

As you are setting up a new account click **Add** and select **Mail...** from the list which appears. Then the Internet Connection Wizard starts up and asks you for the details of your e-mail account, as discussed earlier in this section.

If you have the information to hand it's simply a matter of entering it in the dialogue boxes then clicking **Next**.

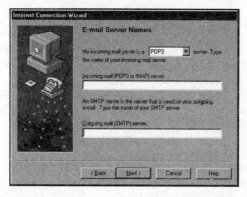

After entering all of your personal information you are asked for your connection type, usually **Connect using my phone line**, but in some cases a LAN (Local Area Network) if you are working in a larger organisation. Finally you are asked to create a new dial-up connection or select an existing one. This includes the telephone number your computer dials for the Internet Service Provider, plus your login name and password.

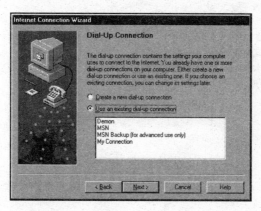

Dial-up Networking is discussed in the previous chapter.

Using Outlook Express

If you've set up your e-mail account with a connection to the Internet, then sending a basic e-mail is easy. You simply enter the e-mail address of the person you are contacting, fill in a short subject, type the message and click the **Send** icon. Of course, there are many more sophisticated features possible with a program like Outlook Express and some of the major ones will be discussed in the next chapter.

First however, we can test the system by sending a simple e-mail message to ourselves. Please note that most of the work is carried out working *offline* in Outlook Express. You only need to go *online*, thereby incurring connection charges, to actually send an e-mail or download your new mail. Downloading involves retrieving your mail from the incoming mail server in the office of the Internet Service Provider and copying to the desktop computer sitting in your home or office. (You can set Outlook Express to work offline using the menu option **File** and **Work Offline**. Or you can click **Cancel** if your machine tries to dial up the ISP after Outlook Express is first launched).

After starting Outlook Express from its icon on the desktop or from **Start**, **Programs**, **Internet Explorer** and **Outlook Express,** you are presented with a panel showing the main options.

Clicking **Compose a Message** gives you a blank page in which to enter your e-mail. To test the system, enter your own e-mail address in the **To:** slot. The **Cc:** and **Bcc:** copies fields can be ignored in this test.

Then enter a short **Subject:** followed by the text of the message in the main panel. To format your mail like a Web page (with fonts, graphics and links to Web sites) select **Format** and **Rich Text (HTML)**.

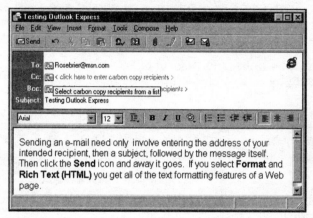

To insert a picture at the position of the cursor, select **Insert**, **Picture...** and **Browse...** to find the graphic on the hard disc. Then click **OK** to insert the graphic.

To insert a hyperlink, type your chosen name for the link, mark it, then select **Insert**, **Hyperlink...** and type the URL for the Web site in the window which appears, then click **OK**. After your e-mail arrives the recipient can use the link to connect directly to the Web site.

When the message is complete, click **Send** at the top left of the screen. This places your outgoing message in the **Outbox** until it has been successfully sent. (The Outbox and other Outlook Express folders can be seen on the next screenshot). Then it is transferred to the **Sent Items** folder where it remains until you delete it.

If you now click **Send and Receive** the computer will dial up the your Internet Service Provider and send the mail to your recipient's incoming mail server (in this example you are the recipient). If the connection is successful, within a short time (almost instantaneously, if you are lucky) your test e-mail to yourself should be downloaded to your computer.

Incoming mail arrives in the **Inbox** as soon as you download your new mail. So you should see your test e-mail in the list - possibly alongside of a list of "spam" or junk mail.

Messages appear in bold until you have opened them to read, by double clicking on their titles in the Inbox.

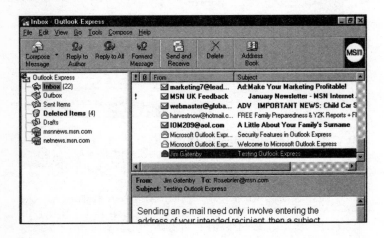

Please note that to read an e-mail which has been created in the HTML format, the recipient must use an e-mail program which supports the MIME (Multipurpose Internet Mail Extensions) standard. Otherwise they will only receive plain text with no fonts, graphics or Internet links.

Responding to Mail

You may wish to read your e-mails then save them in a folder of your choice using **File** and **Save As...** from the Outlook Express menu bar. Or you may wish to obtain a hard copy on paper by printing directly using **File** and **Print**.

Outlook Express also has a set of features which make it easier for you to respond immediately to the original message:

 Reply to Author automatically fills in the sender's return address and includes a copy of the original e-mail so that you can send an instant reply, with your comments.

 Reply to All automatically addresses a reply to the author and all recipients of the original e-mail and includes a copy of the original e-mail and your comments.

 Forward Message sends the message on to the contacts whose e-mail addresses you have entered in the **To:** field.

Deleting Messages

The four folders **Deleted Items**, **Inbox**, **Outbox** and **Sent Items** are integral components of Outlook Express and cannot be deleted. Unwanted items can be removed from any of the folders by selecting the item and pressing the **Delete** key or using the **Delete** icon on the main Outlook Express menu bar.

When you delete an item from the **Inbox**, **Outbox** or **Sent Items** folders in Outlook Express it is moved to the **Deleted Items** folder. However, to remove items permanently from the hard disc, you must then remove them from the **Deleted Items** folder (using the delete key or the **Delete** icon as previously described).

Alternatively you can switch on the option to **Empty messages from the 'Deleted Items' folder on exit** using **Tools**, **Options** and the **General** tab as shown below.

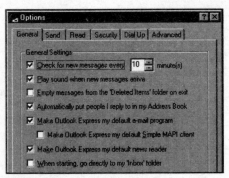

Creating Your Own Mail Folders

If you send or receive a lot of mail which you want to keep for future reference, you'll need to organise it into separate folders. Suppose you communicate socially with friends, receive business messages relating to work, and handle mail in your capacity as secretary of a sub-aqua club. We might therefore wish to create folders called, for example, **Social**, **Business** and **Sub-Aqua** in a folder called **Personal Folders** (which had been created earlier).

To create a new folder, first highlight **Personal Folders**, then **File, Folder** and **New Folder....** (Or click the right button over **Personal Folders**.) Now type the name of the new folder in the resulting window.

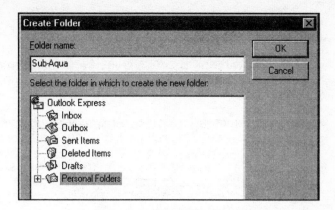

You can then create a hierarchy of sub-folders within the newly created folders, as shown below:

The **File/Folder** menu in Microsoft Outlook Express has the options **Move To...**, **Compact**, **Delete** and **Rename** files and folders. (But not the four permanent Outlook Express folders mentioned earlier.)

Now it's a simple task to drag the mail items from the **Inbox** (for example) and drop them into the new folder that you have created for them. This *moves* (rather than *copies*) the file from its original location. Select **Edit** or click the right button over an e-mail to see the full range of available operations. Incoming mail can be routed into folders of your choice using the **Inbox Assistant** described in the next chapter.

Summary: Outlook Express Basics

- Microsoft Outlook Express is installed when you set up Internet Explorer. It can be removed (or added) in Windows Setup.

- Outlook Express can be used with various Internet Service Providers as well as The Microsoft Network.

- To create a new e-mail account, precise details such as your login name, password, e-mail address and mail server names must be obtained from your Internet Service Provider.

- Most tasks other than the sending and downloading of mail should be carried out *offline* to save Internet connection charges.

- Outlook Express allows message text to be formatted in HTML, like a Web page, with different fonts, graphics and links to Web sites.

- Various facilities simplify the sending of responses to e-mails. These include the automatic in-filling of the addresses of the sender and the original recipients and also the insertion of the text of the original message. E-mails can also be *forwarded*.

- In addition to four permanent mail folders (**Inbox**, **Outbox**, **Sent Items** and **Deleted Items**) you can create additional folders of your own. Messages can be "dropped" into them using the mouse or deposited automatically using the Inbox Assistant.

- Unwanted messages can removed from the **Inbox** using the **Delete** key or the **Delete** icon on the menu bar. To remove them permanently they must be deleted from the **Deleted Items** folder. This can be automated in **Tools**, **Options** and **General**.

4. OUTLOOK EXPRESS FEATURES

The Address Book

This feature can be used to record all of your regular e-mail contacts. Instead of typing in their address every time you send them an e-mail, you just select their name from the list in the Address Book.

You can open the Address Book by clicking on its icon on the top of the Outlook Express window.

Address Book

To make a new entry click **New Contact** and type their details in the **Properties** window which appears.

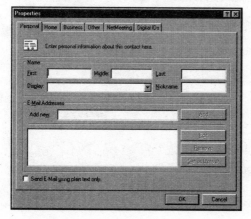

Note that apart from the person's name and e-mail address, you can also store a mass of other information such as their business address and job details and a link to their Web site.

You can also add new contacts to the Address Book by double clicking on one of their messages in the Inbox. This opens up the e-mail in its own window. Then double click on their e-mail address in the **From:** field in the e-mail window and click **Add to Address Book** in the resulting window. There is also an option (**Tools**, **Options**, **General**) to automatically enter people into the Address Book when you reply to them.

Once your Address Book is up and running, it is used when composing a new message. Click on the list icon in the **To:** field to bring up the **Select Recipients** window of the Address Book. Select the names of the people you wish to receive the message and then click **To:** (or **Cc** or **Bcc**) to transfer them into the **Message recipients:** list. Clicking **OK** places the selected contacts in the **To:** field of the new message.

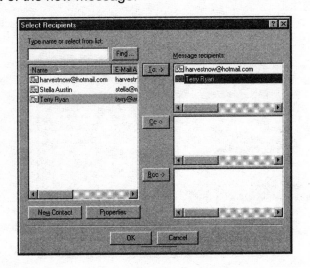

To automate e-mailing further, you can organise your contacts into *groups* using the Address Book. Then when you want to send the same e-mail to everyone, you simply enter the group name instead of every individual contact.

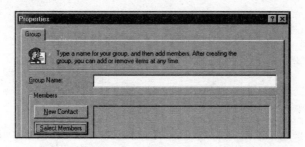

You can also import lists of e-mail contacts from other address books such as those created in the e-mail programs Eudora Pro and Eudora Light.

The Inbox Assistant

The **Inbox Assistant** in Outlook Express is a feature which can be set up to distribute your incoming mail according to a set of rules which you define. These include directing mail from a certain contact into a particular folder, or forwarding it on to another recipient. The rules for the incoming mail are set up in Outlook Express using **Tools**, **Inbox Assistant...** then **Add** as shown on the next page.

When entering the criteria for dealing with the incoming mail, you don't need to type in any e-mail addresses which are listed in your Address Book. Simply click the small hand/list icon in the Inbox Assistant to bring up the Address Book. Highlight the required contacts and click **To** and **OK** to transfer the addresses to the criteria slots in the Inbox Assistant.

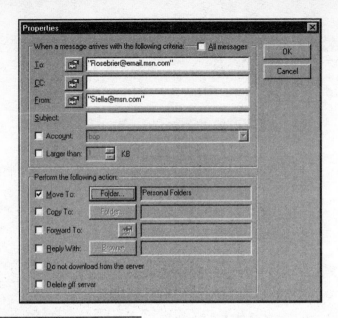

E-mail Attachments

When you send an e-mail message, you can include
with it an additional file as an *attachment*. The file,
selected from your hard disc, might for example be a
word processing document, a spreadsheet, graphics,
sound or video clip. When the file is received, the
attachment appears as an icon below the message. If
you double click the icon, the attached file is opened,
running in its associated program. So, for example, an
attached spreadsheet file might open up in Microsoft
Excel or similar.

I have used this method to send attachments consisting
of about 50 compressed pages of Word text and
graphics, when needed urgently by the printers 130
miles away. The text is delivered to the printer's hard
disc in a few minutes ready for output to a Linotronic
typesetter - compared with several hours or even days
when sending the file on floppy discs by post or courier.

Sending an Attachment

As an example, let's send an e-mail with a graphics file as an attachment. After the e-mail body text has been entered in the normal way, you select **Insert** and **File Attachment:** from the menu bar, as shown below.

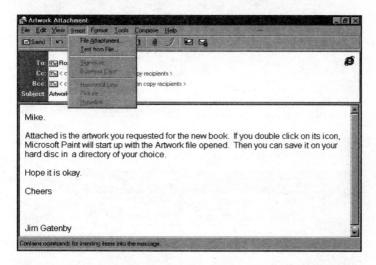

The **Insert Attachment** box opens to allow you to select, from within the hierarchy of folders on your hard disc, the file which is to be attached to the e-mail. Clicking **Attach** inserts an icon for the attachment onto the message.

The e-mail together with the attachment are then sent as a single item. Bear in mind, however, that if the attachment is a substantial file, both the sending and receiving times will be increased compared with a simple e-mail text-only message.

Receiving an Attachment

When the message (together with its attachment) is received into an **Inbox**, the presence of the attachment is shown by a paper clip on the left of the line giving the message details.

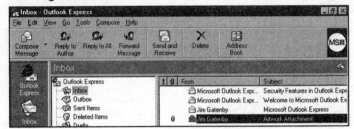

Opening up the message shows the icon for the attachment below the text of the message.

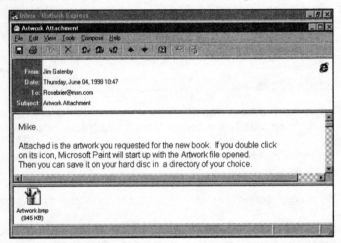

In this example the attachment is a graphic file. Clicking on the icon invokes the following virus warning and gives the opportunity to either open the file or save it to disc.

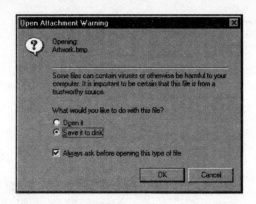

The option **Open it** will open the graphic file, running in its associated program, in this case Microsoft Paint. The attachment can then be saved as a separate file. In this example the attachment could be saved as a .BMP file from within Microsoft Paint.

If you select **Save it to disk** the following box appears to allow you to choose the directory into which the attachment file is to be placed.

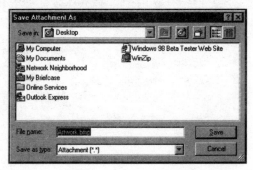

The sending of different types of file as attachments is enabled by the MIME protocol (Multipurpose Internet Mail Extension). This is a system for encoding and decoding files. To accept the attachments you send, the receiving computer must also be using an e-mail package which supports MIME.

Outlook Express Stationery

This is a feature in Outlook Express which allows you to customise your outgoing messages. In effect you create a template, with your own personal details, preferred fonts and perhaps a background pattern. From the main Outlook Express window select **Tools**, **Stationery...** and **Mail**.

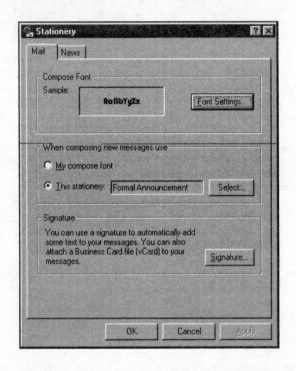

Any changes you make using the **Font Settings...** option will be applied to all new e-mail messages which you compose.

Referring to the Stationery dialogue box shown previously, if you switch on **This stationery:** using the radio button, you can choose from a set of ready-made background patterns and styles.

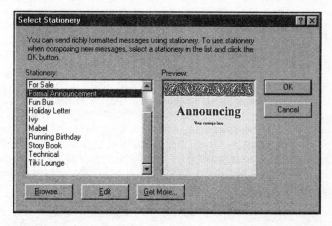

Finally the **Signature...** feature in the Stationery dialogue box allows you to include some personal text, (like your address and telephone number) into all of your e-mails. You can also include a "business card" derived from the business section of the Address Book.

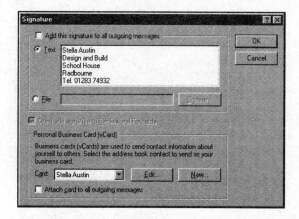

E-mail Security

Outlook Express includes optional security features to ensure that e-mail can only be read by the intended recipients. Also to confirm that it really has been sent by the stated originator. There are two main parts of the security system in Outlook Express - *encryption* and the *digital ID*. Encryption is a process which makes a message unintelligible to all but the intended recipients, for example by re-arranging the letters according to certain rules. The digital ID (or certificate) is an electronic method of proving your identity. It consists of two secret passwords, the *public key* and the *private key*. You can set up the security features in Outlook Express by selecting **Tools**, **Options** and the **Security** tab, and switching on (with a tick) the two options under **Secure Mail**.

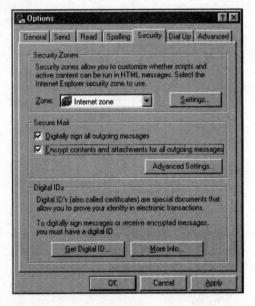

Before you can send encrypted mail and attach a digital signature, you must first obtain your own digital ID.

This process can be launched by clicking **Get Digital ID...** in the **Options** window shown previously. This will take you online to the Microsoft web site containing details of the various independent providers of digital IDs.

Where to Get Your Digital ID   **Outlook**
The following is a list of certifying authorities
from which you can get a digital ID:

VeriSign is Microsoft's preferred provider of digital IDs, and is the leading provider of digital authentication products and services. Through a special offer from VeriSign, Microsoft Internet Explorer 4.0 and Outlook users can obtain a free trial digital ID which you can use to positively identify yourself to, or receive encrypted messages from, business associates, friends, and online services when you use secure e-mail.

Selecting one of these providers will take you to their Web site to set up your digital ID certificate. This will cost a monthly fee and there are some free trial offers.

Choose a Full-service Class 1 Digital ID, or a 60-day Trial Class 1 Digital ID

I'd like a one-year, full-service Digital ID for only US$6.95 per year.	⦿
I'd like to test drive a 60-day trial Digital ID for free. Does not include revocation, replacement, renewal or coverage under the NetSure Protection Plan.	○

Once set up you can use your digital ID to sign your outgoing e-mails to confirm your identity as the genuine sender; also to use encryption for the sending and receiving of private messages.

For someone to send you an encrypted e-mail, they must have your digital ID in their address book - which you can supply simply by sending them a digitally signed message. Your public key enables them to send you an encrypted message. Your private key enables you and you alone to read the message.

Newsgroups and Outlook Express

A newsgroup is formed by a collection of people interested in communicating with others on a particular topic. There are thousands of free newsgroups running discussions on apparently every conceivable subject. Members "post" their contributions to the group using Outlook Express, in a similar way to sending an e-mail. All other subscribers can then view the messages and possibly add to the debate. The quality of the contributions is variable and sadly there is scope for abuse - the content of some newsgroups is monitored.

Your first step towards joining a newsgroup is to click the **Read News** icon in Outlook Express. You then go online to view a list of groups to which you may freely subscribe. On the left of the **Newsgroups** window you can see Read News

the two news servers, msnnews.msn.com and netnews.msn.com.

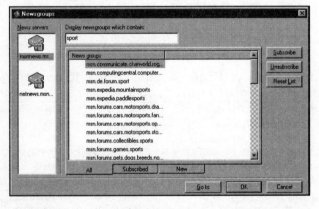

Your choice of newsgroup can be simplified by typing a key word such as "sport" in the **Display newsgroups which contain:** bar. This avoids scrolling through thousands of newsgroup names.

You can have a look at the contributions by selecting a newsgroup and clicking **Go to**. The resulting window is rather like the Inbox for e-mails in Outlook Express.

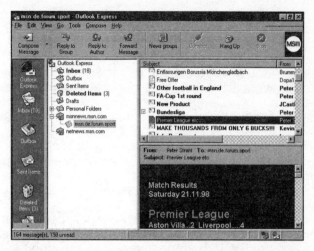

If you wish to join the newsgroup, click **Subscribe** in the main **Newsgroups** window shown on the previous page. This newsgroup is then added to your folders in Outlook Express. Next time you go online to read the news, the newsgroup folder will open

automatically. To send a news message, click **Compose Message**, enter the text and click **Post**.

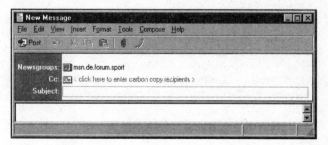

Summary: Outlook Express Features

- The **Address Book** automates the addressing of e-mails and stores contacts' personal and business information including links to their Web site.

- Your regular contacts can be organised into **groups**, facilitating the sending of one message to a lot of different recipients, simply by entering the group name instead of many individual e-mail addresses.

- The **Inbox Assistant** allows you to distribute your incoming mail to a folder of your choice or respond to it according to rules which you set up from a list provided in the **Inbox Properties** dialogue box.

- **Attachments** are files which are "clipped" to an e-mail and sent with it. All types of file can be sent - word processing, spreadsheet and multimedia. The recipient can open the attachment to view in its associated program or save it on their hard disc.

- **Stationery** enables you to customise all of your outgoing e-mails with your chosen font, background pattern and a signature containing personal text.

- **Security** uses encryption to prevent other people from reading your private mail. A Digital ID confirms your identity when you send mail and enables you to read encrypted mail sent to you by other people.

- **Newsgroups** enable people with a common interest to send messages which are "posted" to the news server. All other members of the newsgroup can read the messages and contribute to the debate if they wish. Subscription to a newsgroup is free and there are thousands to choose from.

5. EUDORA PRO

Eudora Pro from Qualcomm is an example of an e-mail *client.* In the computing context, the client software is that installed on the computer of the ordinary person or "end user". This contrasts with the *server* software installed on the host computers, used to manage the Internet service. Online Services such as America Online and CompuServe have their own integral e-mail software. So Eudora Pro would typically be installed by Windows 98 users who have chosen to subscribe to an Internet Service Provider like Demon and Virgin.

There are two versions, Eudora Pro and Eudora Light. Light is a complete e-mail program and is available free by downloading from the Internet. Eudora Pro is a very popular yet inexpensive e-mail package and can be purchased from the usual software suppliers. At the time of writing version 4.0 is being supplied on CD, with an upgrade to version 4.1 available as a download from the Internet at:

http://www.eudora.com

Installing Eudora Pro

To use Eudora Pro you must already have a dial-up connection to the Internet through an Internet Service Provider such as Demon or Virgin. Inserting the CD in its drive launches the set up procedure automatically. This is a straight forward process and includes the option to install a number of components.

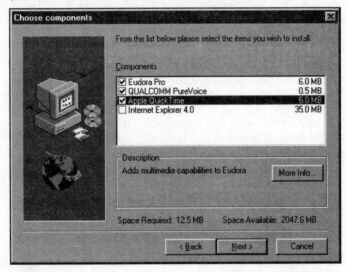

QUALCOMM PureVoice is a component which allows voice messages to be included along with an e-mail. Apple QuickTime is a multimedia program enhancing the display of graphics within the text of an e-mail. (Internet Explorer 4 is, of course, included free on the Windows 98 CD).

After clicking **Next** and copying the files for the various components, **Eudora Pro** should appear on the **Start** and **Programs** menu shown on the next page.

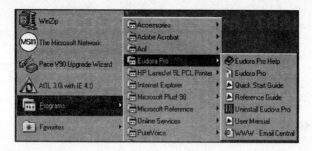

The first time you invoke Eudora Pro from the menu you will be presented with the **New Account Wizard** which allows you to create a new mail account or import the settings from an existing one.

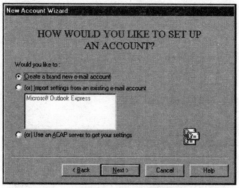

If you are creating a new account you will need to supply accurate and important pieces of information:

The following information is requested by Eudora:

Your Name

Your name as you would like it to appear in the **From:** field on e-mail messages.

E-Mail Address

The return address for your incoming mail assigned to you by, or agreed with, your Internet Service Provider.

e.g.   **jim@gatenby.demon.co.uk**

Login Name

The unique name which you use to log in to the Internet, arranged with your Internet Service Provider.

Incoming Mail Server

The name of the computer at your Internet Service Provider, which deals with your incoming mail (normally a "pop" server).

e.g.   **pop3.demon.co.uk**

You need to have this information readily to hand before you start setting up Eudora Pro. Any missing items should be obtained by phoning your Internet Service Provider. Accuracy is essential, so all details should be carefully written down in a safe place for future reference. After completing the Eudora New Account Wizard you are ready to run Eudora for the first time. It should be possible to launch **Eudora Pro** from the **Start** and **Progams** menu as previously described and to send yourself a test message. (If this doesn't work initially you can always check and modify the settings from within the Eudora program.)

Sending an E-mail

Eudora Pro starts up by default with a daily tip, which can be switched off if desired.

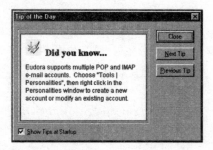

The main screen shows all of the facilities of Eudora Pro as a powerful e-mail client with three main windows **In**, **Out** and **Trash**.

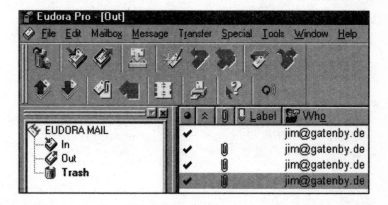

To send a test e-mail to yourself, start a new message by clicking on **Message** then **New Message**. Alternatively click the **New Message** icon as shown on the right.

Enter your own e-mail return address in the **To:** field. Note that Eudora Pro automatically completes the **From:** field.

Enter a suitable **Subject:** and compose a short message in the blank panel below. You can see that Eudora Pro has many of the features of a word processor, selected by icons across the top of the new message panel. These include various fonts, bold, italic and text formatting such as centred and justified.

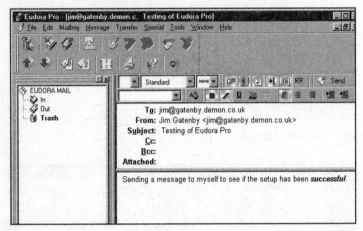

When you are happy with the message text click on the **Send** icon on the top right. Then your modem should dial up your Internet Service Provider and send the message. At this point the message should have been moved to the **Out** tray, verifiable by double clicking the **Out** icon.

Receiving New Mail

After a few moments you should be able to see if the e-mail has arrived at your incoming mail server by clicking on the **Check Mail** icon or selecting **File** and **Check Mail** from the menus.

You will be asked to enter the password which you have arranged with your Internet Service Provider.

If you enter the wrong password you will be informed on the screen that Eudora Pro was unable to connect to the mail server.

However, all being well you should see the more welcome announcement "**You have new mail!**" and the test e-mail should appear when you open up the **In** tray by clicking on its icon.

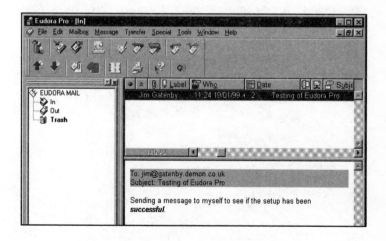

Troubleshooting

If your e-mail failed, the problem is likely be either the connection to your Internet Service Provider or the details of your e-mail account. You can check the connection to the ISP in **My Computer** and **Dial-Up Networking**. Double clicking on the name of the appropriate connection should dial up the number and get you online to your Internet Service Provider.

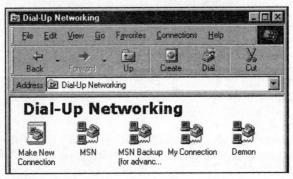

Failure with the Dial-Up may be caused by a faulty connection telephone number for the ISP, or it may simply be very busy.

This can be checked by speaking to the ISP support staff (by old-fashioned telephone), at the help-desk telephone number which should have been provided when you originally signed up for the Internet service.

You can check details of your e-mail account in Eudora Pro by selecting **Tools** and **Options...**. The resulting **Options** window displays the various settings, selected by the **Category:** icons down the left hand side. **Getting Started**, **Checking Mail**, **Incoming Mail** and **Sending Mail** show the e-mail settings.

These settings should be carefully noted before telephoning the support technicians of the Internet Service Provider. Any corrections can be made by altering the contents in the various **Options** windows as shown in the **Getting Started** window above.

Many of the operations in Eudora Pro can be launched by clicking the appropriate icon in the menu bar across the top of the window. Some of the most important icons are shown on the next page. Not shown are the icons to check spelling, print, obtain help and to launch the voice message program PureVoice.

The Eudora Pro Menu Bar

 Delete a message

 Open the **In** mailbox

 Open the **Out** mailbox

 Check the mail (Download new mail to your computer)

 Compose a new message

 Reply to a message - the **To:** field is automatically addressed to the original sender.

 Reply to all recipients and the sender of a message - the **To:** field is automatically filled.

 Forward an e-mail to another address (to be entered). Original e-mail is included in the text.

 Redirect a message to a new address, **From:** as per original sender, by way of your address.

 Attach, to the e-mail, a file from your hard disc such as a Word, Excel or graphics file.

 Open an Address Book

Eudora Pro formats text in the HTML language with all of the features of a Web page - text in different fonts and colours with embedded graphics.

It is also possible for a message to contain hyperlinks which a recipient of your e-mail can click to go direct to a particular Internet Web site.

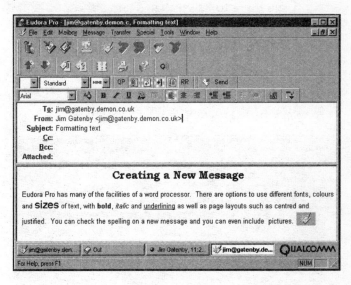

Clicking on the **Attach File** icon allows you to select a file from your hard disc to attach to an e-mail.

Eudora Pro has many other features, such as the creation of electronic address books for your regular contacts.

The next section looks at QUALCOMM PureVoice, a component of Eudora Pro which allows you to enhance your e-mail with a voice message. You might, for example, wish to add a spoken greeting to friends or relatives across the globe, which is more personal than the text in the e-mail **In** box.

QUALCOMM PureVoice

This is a component of Eudora Pro which enables you to record a voice message and send it with your e-mail. You need a sound card, speakers and microphone to prepare the message and the recipient needs a sound card and speakers to listen to it. They also need a copy of the PureVoice Player-Recorder software which can be downloaded free from the Internet at:

http://www.eudora.com

When you buy Eudora Pro on CD, you are given the option to install PureVoice in the initial setup.

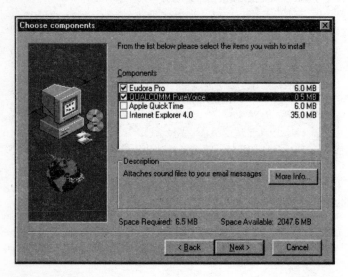

Once installed QUALCOMM PureVoice can be launched by clicking on its icon on the lower right of the Eudora Pro menu bar.

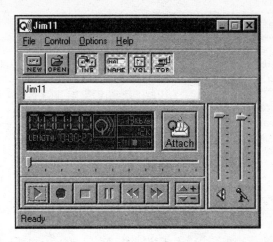

Simply click the record button and speak the message into the microphone. Then you can either save the message as a voice file in a folder of your choice on the hard disc, or you can click **Attach** to clip the voice file directly to your e-mail message.

After you send the e-mail, the recipient downloads the new message together with the voice mail file. The voice file is represented by an icon (shown right) at the bottom of the message.

Clicking on this icon launches the QUALCOMM PureVoice Player-Recorder allowing the recipient to play the voice message.

EUDORA WEB-MAIL

There is a free e-mail service, **Eudora Web-Mail** sponsored by advertising. Being web-based makes it easy to check your e-mail from different locations anywhere in the world. All you need is a computer with a connection to the Internet. You can sign up at:

http://www.eudora.com

Summary: Eudora Pro

- Eudora Pro is an e-mail program used by subscribers to Internet Service Providers such as Demon Internet, rather than the Online Services like America Online and The Microsoft Network.

- Eudora Pro allows mail to be formatted in HTML in the style of a Web page with fonts, colours and URLs providing hyperlinks to the World Wide Web.

- Eudora Light is a version of the Eudora software available free by downloading from the Internet.

- Before installing Eudora Pro, you must have a connection to the Internet via an Internet Service Provider or Online Service. This will provide you with a login name, password, e-mail return address and the details of the mail server computers.

- Important settings can be modified after the initial installation using **Tools** and **Options:**

- The Eudora Pro CD includes the Apple QuickTime software to support the use of graphics in e-mails.

- QUALCOMM PureVoice is a component of Eudora Pro which allows voice messages to be recorded, played and sent with e-mails.

- Eudora Web-Mail is a free e-mail service giving easy access regardless of geographical location.

- The latest versions of the Eudora software can be downloaded from:

http://www.eudora.com

6. VOICE MAIL

Introduction

For little or no additional expense, your computer can become the centre of a complete communications system. One small voice modem, physically no bigger than this book, can streamline your desktop by replacing bulky devices such as an answerphone and a fax machine. In *speakerphone* mode you can carry on working "hands free", speaking into a microphone and listening to replies coming from a loudspeaker.

This computerised "messaging" system is integrated within Windows 98 and can run in the background (minimised on the Task Bar), while you carry on with word processing or whatever. (Modems like the Pace 56 Solo have on-board memory which allows them to record messages even when the computer is switched off.) A voice modem can distinguish between incoming voice and fax messages and these are saved as files on the hard disc. Voice files can be copied, moved or deleted in a similar way to document files produced in other applications such as Word, etc.

You can also create a large number of "mailboxes" for different people in a family, business or school, etc. Incoming voice and fax messages are routed to the correct mailbox using an answerphone menu system ("Press 1 for Sales...", etc.) If you're travelling away from home, you can use a telephone to dial into your computer and play your voice messages.

If you already have a computer and internal voice modem, the only additional expense might be a pair of speakers and possibly a microphone, which can be bought for a few pounds. With an external voice modem, even these may not be essential, since perfectly acceptable quality may be produced using the speaker and microphone built into the modem.

Voice Software

If your computer system came with a modem already fitted, the voice software may be set up and listed on the **Programs** menu accessed off **Start**. When you buy a voice modem separately, the package normally includes software to manage the voice and fax facilities. The last two modems I have bought came with the SuperVoice software from Pacific Image Communications. It is installed simply by inserting the CD and following the on-screen instructions which appear automatically.   The next section uses the SuperVoice software to demonstrate the main features of modern voice messaging systems. (SuperVoice also manages fax communications as discussed later).

The SuperVoice program is invoked by selecting **Start**, **Programs** and **SuperVoice**.

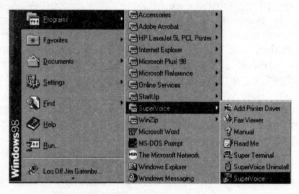

Each time you select the program, SuperVoice runs a check on your modem and communications port.

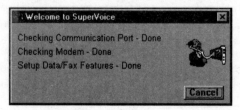

Then you are presented with **Dialer**, a window containing a virtual telephone from which you can operate the voice and fax systems.

Transmitting Voice Messages

You can use your voice modem to make conventional telephone calls. Either use the microphone built into the modem or, if necessary to improve quality, connect a microphone to the **MIC** socket on the modem. Similarly, you can either use the modem's internal speakers or, alternatively, connect some external speakers to the modem **SPKR** socket.

If your computer is already fitted with a sound card and speakers, you can use these for your voice mail. You may need to change some settings in your voice software if you decide to connect the speakers to the sound card. (SuperVoice uses the .*vox* file type to record sound files whereas sound cards use the .*wav* convention).

The Speed Dialer

Numbers to be dialled can be entered using the
keyboard or by clicking the on-screen key pad. As with
a conventional handset, it's a simple matter to store the
names and numbers of the people you dial regularly.
Click on **Program** in the Dialer window then enter the
names and numbers in the **Program Speed Dialer**.

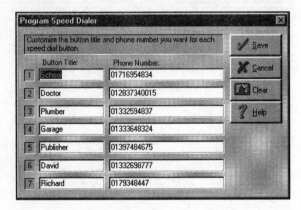

After clicking **Save**, the names will appear on the right
of the main Dialer window.

To make a call, select the button to the left of the
required name and click the **Dial** button.

The Phone Book

SuperVoice provides an electronic phone book, accessed by the **Ph. Book** button on the Dialer window.

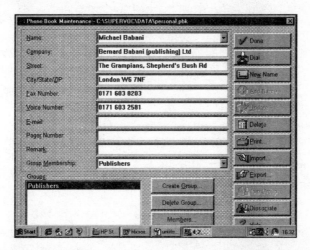

This is particularly useful for fax work discussed later, when it can be used to send the same fax to a large group of recipients. However, it can also be used for voice mail work to find and dial a number, particularly if you regularly dial a large number of contacts. (Having already used up the available names and numbers in the programmable Speed Dialer). To find a person you simply scroll through the list of names which appears when you click the arrow to the right of the **Name:** field.

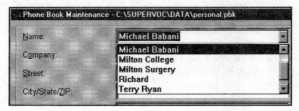

Incoming Messages

Incoming voice (and fax) messages are received into a mailbox. If you are working at the computer when the phone rings you can intercept the call before the answerphone takes over. Selecting the **Sp.Phone** option on the Dialer will allow you to have a two way conversation with the caller. (Provided you have a *full duplex* modem, rather than one of the earlier *half duplex* models).

Mailboxes can be set up for individual users and by default all incoming messages are placed in a mailbox called **Manager**. The previous Dialer window shows that there are currently 3 voice messages waiting in the Manager mailbox.

Clicking on **Messages** at the bottom of the Dialer window reveals the **Incoming Messages** window.

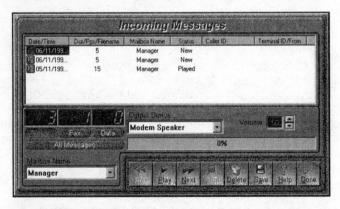

Clicking on **Voice** or **Fax** (or **Data**) allows you to switch between the lists of the various types of message. The above window shows the details of 3 voice messages in the Manager mailbox. The buttons along the bottom of this window allow you to play new messages, delete old ones or save messages in a directory of your choice. (New messages are automatically saved on the hard disc but their location is not obvious). Should you wish to search for the folder containing the messages use **Find** then **Files or Folders** on the **Start** menu. Enter ***.vox** in the **Named:** field to find all voice files and **C:** in the **Look in:** field to search the whole of the hard disc.

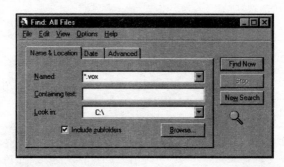

You should find the voice files in the folder **C:\Supervoc**.

From a practical point of view, it's easier to create your own folders with meaningful names and save in them any messages which you wish to retain.

If you select **Save** from the menu in the **Incoming Messages**, you are directed to the **Save As** window open at the **Supervoc\Script1** directory.

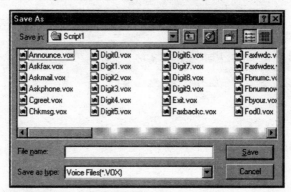

89

This contains all of the default voice messages saved as .vox files. At this point you might wish to select your own folder in which to save any voice messages which have been recorded.

Other mailboxes can be selected by clicking on the arrow to the right of the **Mailbox Name** bar in the Incoming Messages window.

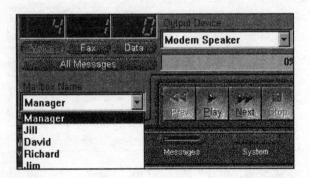

Additionally you can direct the sound output to be played to the speakers via a sound card, rather than through speakers plugged into the modem. This is described in more detail later.

Managing the System

From the Dialer window click on **System** to reveal the main manager menu bar for SuperVoice.

Several of these icons refer to fax messages and are discussed later. **MsgLog** displays the Incoming Messages window described earlier and there is a button to return us to the Dialer window.

The **Voice** option along the top of the **SuperVoice Manager** menu bar contains a number of options for playing and managing voice files.

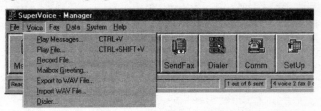

Selecting **Play File...** brings up the directory containing all of the standard messages provided for the answerphone system.

91

You can see that voice messages are saved with the .vox file extension, but in other respects can be treated and managed like other Windows 98 files, using My Computer or the Windows Explorer. You can listen to a message by highlighting the file then clicking **Open**. Then click **Replay** on the window which appears.

You can replace an existing message by recording over the top of it. From the **SuperVoice Manager** menu select **Voice/Record File...**. This brings up the **Save As** dialogue box shown below.

When you select an existing message in the above dialogue box, if you click **Save** you are given the chance to record your own message to replace the old.

SuperVoice Setup

Also provided on the **SuperVoice Manager** menu bar is the **Setup** button.

Clicking **Setup** reveals a further range of buttons with some very important functions.

The **Select Script** button allows you to configure SuperVoice as either a single user answerphone or as a more complex system offering a menu of choices ("Please Press 1 for Sales or 2 for Accounts…", etc.

On clicking **Select Script** the following window appears, in this case with the single user **Answering Machine** option selected.

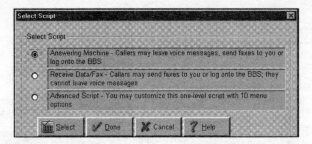

If you now click **Select**, the **Answering Machine Greeting** window appears showing the default answerphone message.

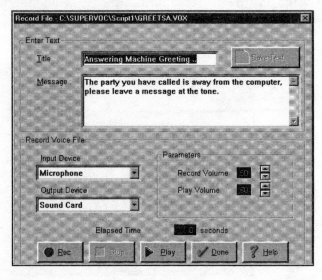

To customise the answerphone with your own personal greeting, simply click **Rec** and speak into the microphone. (You can alter the *text* in the above dialogue box and save it, but any alterations will not affect the words spoken by the answerphone system).

If you select **Advanced Script** in the **Select Script** window shown previously, you are presented with a window which allows you to set up a menu of touchtone options for callers to your system.

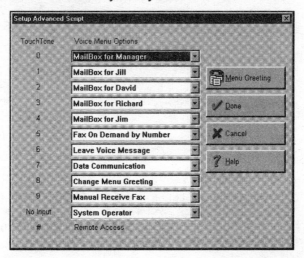

Each of the **TouchTone** numbers down the lefthand side can be programmed to perform different functions. If you click on the right of any of the **Voice Menu Options** a drop down menu presents a range of actions available for each number. These include any mailboxes which you have previously set up (as described in the next section). For example, a caller pressing 3 would be directed into Richard's mailbox.

Setting Up Mailboxes

To create a new mailbox, select **MailBox** from the **Setup Supervoice** window shown below.

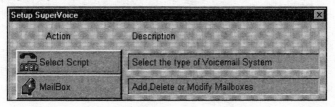

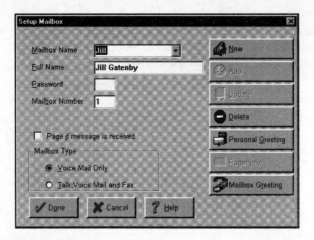

Mailboxes are set up by clicking on **New**, entering the person's details then clicking **Add**. At this point you can record a message which the caller hears when reaching a particular mailbox. Now click on **Personal Greeting** and press **Rec** to record your greeting.

Mailbox Greeting contains a message such as "Press 1 for Sales....". This would be customised by recording a new message as described above.

If you select **Voice Parameters** from the **Setup SuperVoice** window you can alter the times allowed for the various messaging operations.

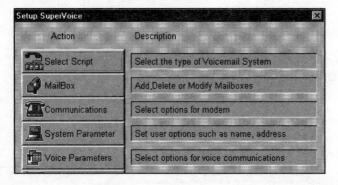

By default these times are kept short to minimise the amount of hard disc space used to store voice messages.

Also shown is the option to switch on **Call Screening**. This allows you to intercept calls before the phone rings and possibly decide to allow the answerphone to take the call. This facility only works if your telephone line has been enabled for **Calling Line Identification** by the telephone company. You must also have a voice modem which supports this service.

A further option, **Sound Card** accessed from **Setup SuperVoice/Modem** allows you to play your voice messages through speakers connected to the sound card rather than the modem. Sound messages in the .vox format used by SuperVoice for saving voice files must be converted to the .wav format compatible with many sound cards.

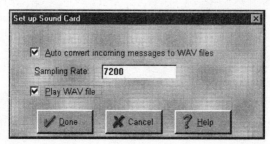

97

Summary: Voice Mail

- A voice modem can save desk space by replacing individual devices like fax machines and telephones.

- Voice messages are saved as files on the hard disc and can be managed (moved, copied, deleted, etc.) in the Windows Explorer.

- Some voice modems can store incoming voice (and fax) messages even when the computer is switched off. Others require the computer to be switched on with the voice software running in the background.

- Voice modems can distinguish between incoming voice and fax messages and store them accordingly.

- Speakerphone mode permits a hands free, two way conversation using a microphone and speakers - without the need for a telephone handset.

- A voice modem can act either as a single-user answerphone or with a spoken TouchTone menu system leading to a large number of mailboxes for individual users.

- The standard greetings which a caller hears on dialling into a voice modem can easily be replaced by personal greetings recorded by the user.

- A voice modem may have a built-in microphone and speaker which give acceptable quality. Alternatively voice messages can be played through external speakers connected either to the modem or to the computer's sound card.

- Voice software like SuperVoice allows the user to program frequently-dialled names and numbers onto buttons on the screen. You can also compile an electronic phone book for rapid telephony and fax.

7. VIDEO CONFERENCING WITH NETMEETING

Video conferencing is a method of communicating across a network, which attempts to emulate a face-to-face meeting between people in the same room. Although the technology is still in its infancy, the basic elements of a meeting - seeing other people and holding a discussion with the help of visual aids - are already possible. If you have access to a Windows 98 (or Windows 95) computer, connected to the Internet, then you can start video conferencing with very little additional expense.

Windows 98 has its own conferencing program, **Microsoft NetMeeting**. To make use of its *audio* facilities your computer should be fitted with a sound card, speakers and microphone. Most PCs are now fitted with these but if not, perfectly adequate components should be available locally for a few pounds. However, to utilise NetMeeting's *video* conferencing ability, so that people involved in a meeting can see each other, both computers need to be equipped with a video camera. (If your machine doesn't have a camera fitted it can still *receive* live video from a computer which has).

Although professional systems are expensive, you can buy complete video conferencing packages for the home or small business for less than a hundred pounds. Packages normally consist of a camera, video conferencing software and possibly a modem. The camera just plugs in to one of the ports on the back of the computer and is easy to set up, without requiring any special skills. The quality of the video output on these cheap systems is quite rudimentary but it's good enough for you to see the person(s) at the other end. This could enhance a telephone conversation between friends or relatives separated by thousands of miles.

Microsoft NetMeeting is a complete video conferencing program and it's provided free on the Windows 98 CD (although it may still need to be installed onto your hard disc). Even if you don't have a camera fitted you can still use NetMeeting's many other non-video facilities to hold "meetings" with friends and colleagues and exchange notes and information. This could reduce the amount of travelling to meetings.

Microsoft NetMeeting includes the following features:

- Voice communication across the Internet, using microphones and speakers.

- Live video between computers fitted with cameras.

- A "chat" facility enabling an interactive exchange of typed messages between several people.

- A universal Whiteboard which allows meeting "attendees" to make spontaneous contributions to a shared drawing or chart.

- The ability to share applications (like Word or Excel), and to produce a document in collaboration.

- The ability to send files between members of the "meeting".

Installing Microsoft NetMeeting

Before installing NetMeeting, make sure your sound system and camera are working correctly. If **NetMeeting** has already been installed on your hard disc, it will be present on the **Internet Explorer** menu accessed off **Start** and **Programs**.

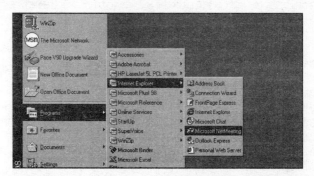

If Microsoft NetMeeting is not listed, it needs to be installed from your original Windows 98 CD. Put the CD in the drive and open up the **Control Panel** from **Start** and **Settings**. Now double click on **Add/Remove** programs and select the **Windows Setup** tab. Next select **Communications** and the **Details...** button. Make sure the box to the left of **Microsoft NetMeeting** is ticked and click **OK** to install the program.

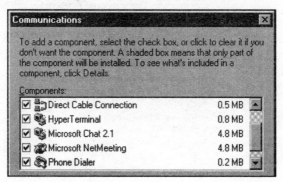

Setting Up NetMeeting

Before using NetMeeting for the first time you need to complete a short setup procedure. This tailors NetMeeting to your computer and to your personal preferences. If you are not sure of the correct response to a request for information you can accept the default settings which Windows 98 provides. These are not "set in stone" - you can alter them later if necessary.

The first decision is which *directory server* to use. The default server is **ils.microsoft.com**. You are advised to accept this initially but you can change it later if you wish. (For example, if you are unable to log on because the directory server is too busy). You can also change directory server to see who is logged on and call them for a meeting.

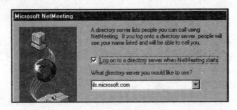

Then you are required to enter your personal details including your e-mail address.

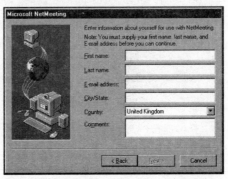

The **Comments** box might be used for a short note to describe the type of work you are involved in or your personal interests.

The next window allows you to select a *category* for your information. If you select **For business use**, for example, other business users will be able to contact you more easily through the directories. It is possible to display the names and e-mail addresses of those logged on to a particular server. In addition you can limit the display of users to those in a particular category e.g. business users. If your system is used by children or you wish to avoid contact with users offering "entertainment" you are advised to select the business category at this stage.

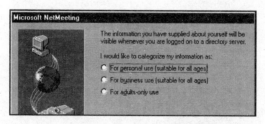

Next you are asked to specify your method of connection (modem, etc.) to the Network. Windows 98 ought to detect the device installed in your particular machine so it should just be a case of accepting this.

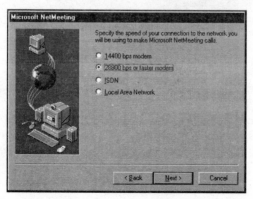

If you have a video camera fitted, this will be detected. You can also select a different device, if necessary, from the drop down menu.

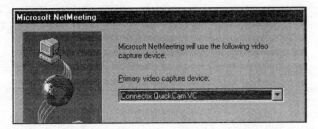

You then enter the audio tuning wizard which allows you to set up your speakers and microphone. The window for testing and adjusting the speaker volume (with a slider) is shown below. A similar window is provided to adjust the microphone.

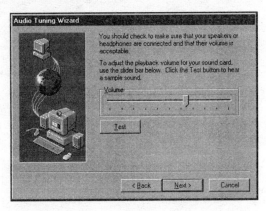

When you have finished tuning the audio system the setup of NetMeeting is complete. You can return to the audio tuning wizard later if you find you need to make adjustments while making a call. The next section deals with running NetMeeting, calling up other users and holding a "meeting".

Starting a NetMeeting Session

The program is invoked from **Start**, **Programs**, **Internet Explorer** and **Microsoft NetMeeting**.

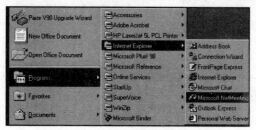

This should lead you onto the Internet, although, depending on your particular configuration, you may need to click a button to start the connection. All being well, the directory server will be found and the main NetMeeting window shown on the next page will be displayed.

If you are unable to connect to a directory server it is probably because your default server is busy. This can be changed in NetMeeting by selecting **Tools**, **Options...** and **Calling**. Alternatively you can reach the same dialogue box using **Call**, **Change My Information...** and **Calling**. I have always been able to log on after trying no more than two or three different directory servers.

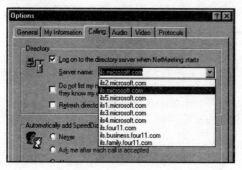

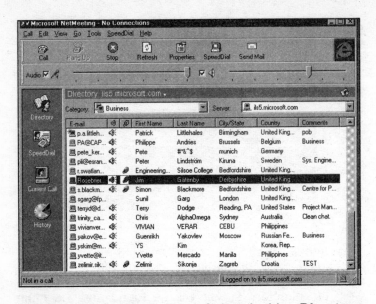

The four icons down the left hand side, **Directory**, **SpeedDial**, **Current Call** and **History**, control what is displayed in the main panel. The NetMeeting window above shows the result of selecting **Directory**. This displays all of the users currently logged on to that directory server. If you want to look at users logged on to another directory, this can be changed by clicking the down arrow to the right of the **Server:** bar. Then select another server from the drop down menu.

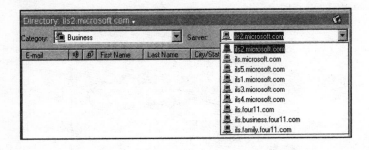

Referring to the main **Directory** panel at the top of the previous page, you can see the personal details entered by users when NetMeeting was first set up.

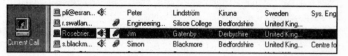

The icons to the right of the e-mail address show whether or not a user's machine has sound or video camera facilities or both. The status bar along the bottom of the main NetMeeting window on the previous page shows the directory server currently logged on to and whether or not you are involved in a call.

You can choose to display only those users who fall into a certain category, such as those with a video camera fitted or those not currently involved in a call. This is achieved by selecting form the drop down menu displayed when you click the down arrow to the right of the **Category:** bar.

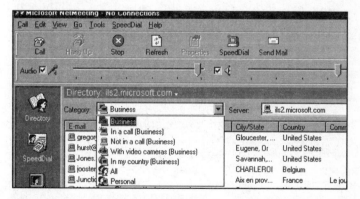

You can also see, across the top of the above window, tick boxes which show that the computer has microphone and speaker facilities and there are sliders to adjust the volume.

The next section looks at the ways to make a call in order to hold a meeting with another user. Before doing so you may wish to check your video camera and make any adjustments. (This can be done by running NetMeeting off-line, i.e. without connecting to the Internet). If you click **Current Call** on the left of the main window, you should see a panel similar to the following.

Initially the panel will show two pictures of the NetMeeting logo; clicking the arrow below the top picture should change the picture to a video of yourself. At the same time the text below it should change from **Not Sending** to **Previewing**.

Making a Call

To call up another user you must both have NetMeeting running and be logged on to a directory server. If you intend to have a meeting with a friend or colleague you would need to agree a time to be simultaneously up and running. Alternatively you can look for people in the directories and call them up. They can choose either to accept or ignore your call. If you do not wish to receive any calls there is a **Do Not Disturb** option which can be set in the **Edit** menu on the main NetMeeting window.

The are several ways to call up another person:

Double click their name in the **Directory** panel list or in the list of your previous contacts in the **SpeedDial** or **History** lists. People you call are automatically added to the SpeedDial, which also tells you if they are currently on line. The History panel logs people who call you and records whether you accepted or ignored the call.

Alternatively click the **Call** telephone icon or select **Call** and **New Call...** from the **NextMeeting** menu bar. Then type their e-mail address into the **New Call** dialogue box which appears.

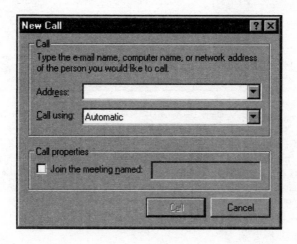

Assuming your intended contact is logged on to a NetMeeting directory server and has not clicked **Do Not Disturb**, the "phone" will ring and a window will appear on their screen giving them the choice to accept or reject your call.

After clicking the **Accept** button the meeting begins. Calls received are logged in the History list which can be viewed by clicking the **History** icon on the left of the main NetMeeting window. To display the video of both yourself and your caller select **Current Call**.

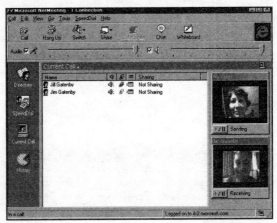

If a picture does not appear in one of the picture frames, you or your contact may need to click the arrow at the bottom left of the picture frames. NetMeeting can be set to send and receive video automatically at the start of a call using the **Video** tab in **Tools** and **Options...**. Sliders in the main NetMeeting window allow you to adjust the volume of the speakers and microphone during a call.

The Whiteboard

This is one of the features of NetMeeting you can use even if you or your contacts don't have video cameras fitted. In some ways the Whiteboard is better than the traditional visual aids used in a physical meeting between people in the same room. The Whiteboard is like an electronic flip chart, with multiple pages, which all the parties to a meeting can see and work on simultaneously. The Whiteboard is started by clicking its icon on the **Current Call** panel of NetMeeting.

The Whiteboard has many of the features of a program like Windows Paint, with the ability to draw lines and shapes and write text. Explanations can be assisted by the use of a pointing hand and diagrams and text can be saved and printed. You can prepare more complex diagrams using the Whiteboard off-line, before going on-line to discuss the work with colleagues at remote locations. Each participant can make changes and these appear on both screens at the same time.

NetMeeting Chat

Only two people can take part in the exchange of audio and video at any one time. The **Chat** feature allows the exchange of *typed notes* between more than two people. When you type a message and press **Enter** your text appears on everyone else's screen. At the end of a session the collection of notes can be saved and printed - making an accurate set of minutes of the meeting. There is also a **Send to:** option to restrict a private message to only one member of a meeting, by selecting their name from the drop down list in the **Send to:** bar at the bottom of the **Chat** window.

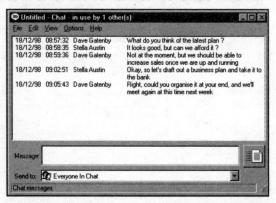

The name of the "speaker", and the date and time of each contribution to the meeting can be switched on or off in **Options**, **Chat Format...**.

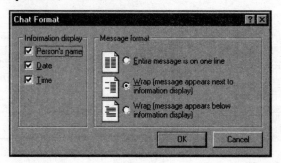

112

Sharing Applications

There may be times when the members of a meeting want to look at a document which has been created in an application such as Word. With the meeting up and running, you open the document in the application. Now minimise the application onto the Taskbar and then, with the **Current Call** panel of NetMeeting open, click the **Share** icon then select the application to be shared from the drop down list.

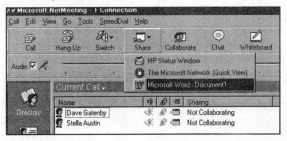

An *image* of the document running in the application will now be available to all members of the meeting. However, sharing does not allow the other members of the meeting to work on the document. To achieve this, all members of the meeting must click on the **Collaborate** icon in the top of the NetMeeting window.

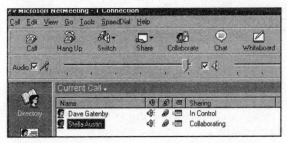

It is also possible to send applications files between participants using **Tools**, **File Transfer**, **Send File....**.

Summary: Video Conferencing with NetMeeting

- Microsoft NetMeeting supports communication using video, voice, typed messages and shared drawings.

- NetMeeting is a Windows 98 component, but may need to be installed from the CD to your hard disc.

- To initiate a meeting, you log onto a directory server, then call up the person you wish to meet with - who may choose to accept or ignore your call.

- NetMeeting may be used socially across the Internet, enabling you to see and speak to friends and relatives who may be thousands of miles away.

- In a business context, NetMeeting allows you to hold formal meetings across a company Intranet or the Internet. Many of the facilities of a conventional meeting are available, reducing the need to travel.

- The Chat facility permits the exchange of typed messages, which can be saved and printed.

- The Whiteboard is like a shared electronic flip chart with drawing facilities, on which everyone can draw and type. The work can be saved and printed.

- Applications software, such as wordprocessors and spreadsheets can be shared between the members of a meeting. The collaborate feature allows several people to work on a joint document.

- Currently NetMeeting only permits video and audio communication between two members of a meeting. You can switch the sound and video link to a different member of the meeting.

- Even without a camera, you can still use the audio facility, Chat, Whiteboard and shared applications.

8. MICROSOFT CHAT

Introduction

Chat is a method of communicating across the Internet and has several features distinguishing it from the techniques discussed earlier in this book. Chat is interactive and involves people "talking" to each other by entering text in short sentences. Chat works in "real-time" - all the participants must be online while the chat is taking place.

There are several major networks managing the chat medium around the world, and these are collectively referred to as Internet Relay Chat (IRC). Well-known networks include EFnet, Undernet, IRCnet and DALnet and each has tens of thousands of users. The networks have a number of *chat servers*; these are computers around the world which play host to the chat sessions.

You can communicate with users on a different server on the same network, but there is no communication between the various networks.

Some of the Online Services schedule chats at certain times. These might provide, for example, a forum for debate about a sporting event, a special interest topic or a discussion with a celebrity.

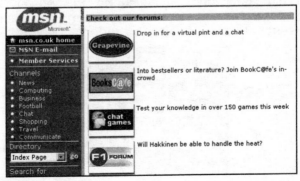

Each server contains a number of chat *channels* (or *rooms* in Microsoft terminology) which people enter to join a conversation. Rooms are often based on a common theme although there are some which are more of a free for all. You may converse with all of the people in a room or you can choose to communicate with one or more selected users - a process known as "whispering".

Chat rooms are often monitored by an operator or host to maintain reasonable standards. There are strict rules for chat (known as "netiquette") and anyone not obeying may be expelled by the operator. While this is obviously intended to prevent offensive behaviour you can also be "kicked" off for seemingly trivial offences like using all capital letters in your sentences. (This is regarded as "shouting"). There is also an option to ignore someone who is annoying you. Chat is based around text messages and there is a set of commands and acronyms to minimise keyboard work. For example, **BBL** is used for Be Back Later and **:-)** is an "emoticon" which represents smiling.

In order to join a chat session you need a *chat client*, a program on your computer which manages the sending and receiving of text. Windows 98 includes its own free chat client, Microsoft Chat. This provides a graphical user interface with a choice between sentences appearing as lines of text or in "balloons" as part of a comic strip. Each user has to choose a unique nickname before starting a session and select a personal character if using the cartoon option.

Installing Microsoft Chat

The software is a component of Windows 98 and therefore arrives free on the Windows 98 CD. Microsoft Chat may have been included in the original installation of Windows 98 on your machine, in which case you will see it on the menu by selecting **Start**, **Programs** and **Internet Explorer**.

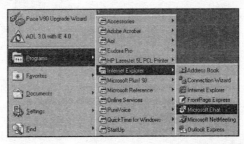

If **Microsoft Chat** is not listed, place your Windows 98 CD in the drive and start the **Windows Setup** procedure. This can be launched from **Start**, **Settings**, **Control Panel**, **Add/Remove Programs** and the **Windows Setup** tab. Select **Communications** and **Details...** and make sure **Microsoft Chat** is ticked as shown below.

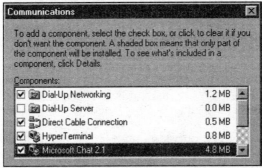

Click **OK** to install Microsoft Chat on the menu system.

Using Microsoft Chat

The program can be invoked by selecting **Start**, **Programs**, **Internet Explorer** and **Microsoft Chat** as previously described. You will be presented with the **Chat Connection** window as shown below.

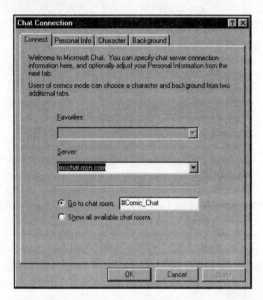

Note that the **Server:** bar already contains the name of a Microsoft server, **mschat.msn.com** and a chat room **#Comic_Chat**. It's the convention for the names of chat rooms (or *channels* on non-MSN servers) to be preceded by the **#** sign. You should find a few servers already available on the drop down **Server:** menu and there are lots more available on the Web sites of the main chat networks.

Further details about finding chat servers are given later in this chapter but you can have a first look at the chat medium using the server names already provided in Microsoft Chat.

Before connecting to a chat server, you can enter information about yourself after selecting the **Personal Info** tab in the Chat Connection window.

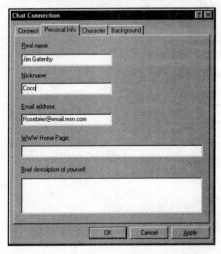

Details such as your name and e-mail address are picked up automatically by the system. Nicknames are usually informal and you can change them and the other personal details afterwards if you wish. The nickname should be unique - it's no good entering "Jim" if someone else is already using it.

Clicking the **Character** tab in the Chat Connection window allows you to select the cartoon character which will represent you in the optional comic strip format shown on the next page.

The circle of faces allows you to select the facial expression for your character and the **Background** tab provides a choice of scenery for your strip.

Having completed all of the personal settings, click **Apply** and **OK** to start dialling the chat server. Once you are connected you should see the optional **Message of the Day** announcing statistics of users, servers, channels (rooms) and operators.

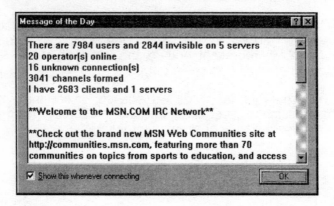

Click **OK** to enter the selected chat room and you can then watch the proceedings to get the gist of the chat - before joining in if you wish.

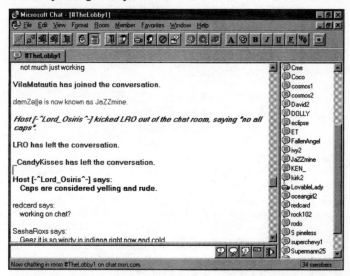

You can change between the text and cartoon strip formats using the icons on the main toolbar.

To join the conversation, type your message in the strip at the bottom of the window and press **Enter**. Your comments appear on the screen immediately.

Regular users of Internet Relay Chat have developed a set of abbreviations to save typing and add feeling to otherwise unemotional text. Some of the main ones are listed below:

AFK	Away from the keyboard
BBL	Be back later
BFN	Bye for now
BRB	Be right back
\<g\>	Grin
\<bg\>	Big grin
\<s\>	Smile
\<bs\>	Big smile
FAQ	Frequently asked question
GMTA	Great minds think alike
LOL	Laugh Out Loud
ROFL	Roll on the floor laughing

Although Microsoft Chat has cartoon characters whose facial expressions can be changed on screen using the mouse, you can also express feelings in text messages by typing "emoticons", for example:

:-) Smiling face

:-(Unhappy face

:-/ Frowning face

;-) Wink

:-P Poking tongue out

Text messages can be formatted in different fonts, italics, etc., using the icons on the right of the toolbar, shown below.

If you want to chat privately to one or more people select their name(s) from the list of users down the right hand side of the screen, then select **Member** and **Whisper Box** or use the icon on the toolbar. The names of the people in the private conversation are shown across the top of the Whisper Box.

Text is entered in the bar at the bottom as before and the conversation appears in the panel above.

If, when you were starting your chat session, you entered the name of a server but didn't enter a chat room in the Chat Connection window when first connecting, you would be presented with a list of all of the rooms on that server.

You can also view the list of rooms (below) while in a chat session using **Room** and **Room List...** from the menu bar or click its icon on the toolbar, shown right.

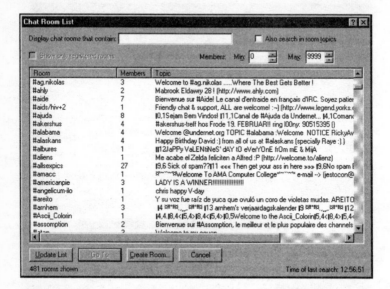

There are icons on the toolbar for entering and leaving rooms and for creating a new room where you can be the operator.

The **User List** shows all of the people currently logged on in all of the various rooms. To see the list click **Member** and **User List...** or click the icon on the toolbar, shown right.

The User List is shown on the next page.

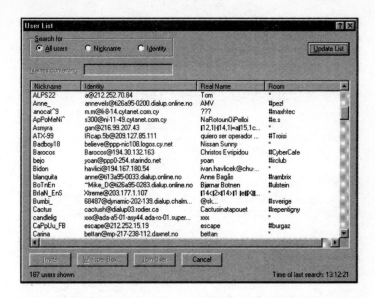

Finding Out More

As described earlier, the names of a few chat servers are provided by default in Microsoft Chat and if you wish you can log on to the server without naming a chat room by selecting **Show all available chat rooms**.

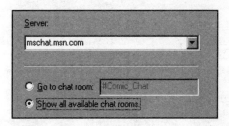

However, in order to find out the names of more chat rooms you might try logging on to the home page of your Internet Service Provider such as MSN or Demon Internet.

These may also provide notes for beginners about Internet Relay Chat and list the names of servers which can be entered into the Chat Connection window described earlier in this chapter. For example, Demon provide two different servers, one on the IRCnet chat network and the other on Efnet. These are:

ircnet.demon.co.uk

efnet.demon.co.uk

Type one of these names into the **Server:** bar in the Chat Connection window and switch on **Show all available chat rooms**.

A useful Web site to look for the names of other chat servers and rooms (or channels) and for general help on chatting is :

http://www.irchelp.org/irchelp/networks/

This site gives a wealth of information for new chat users and also lists the names of channels or rooms on the main chat networks. If you access this Web site and select The Undernet, for example, then click **Servers** you will find the names of a large number of chat servers.

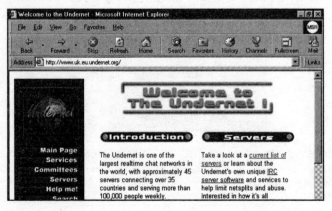

Enter the name of your nearest server into the Chat Connection window discussed previously and switch on the radio button **Show all available chat rooms**. This will allow you to connect to the server and choose a channel (or room) from the list currently available.

The Microsoft Network (http://msn.co.uk/) makes it very easy to access chats on a wide variety of topics. You can have a look at the text of previous conversations with celebrities or you can read the notes on **How to Chat**.

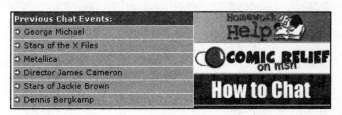

From the same Web page you can set up your own personal chat room, by entering your **Nickname**, **Room name** and clicking **Create**.

MSN also provides a series of chats with technical experts, scheduled for different times of the day.

16:00 - Windows 95/98 Chat
Get the scoop on Windows 95/98 in this moderated chat Monday through Friday.
18:00 - Monthly XML Chat Chat with Microsoft technology experts about XML.
22:00 - Windows 95/98 Technical Chat Join this technical hour for power users of Windows 95/98.

Computing Central, the site for free computing answers from friendly experts.

Summary: Microsoft Chat

- Chat is an interactive method of communication over the Internet, using typed sentences which typically receive an immediate response.

- Internet Relay Chat (IRC) is a series of discrete networks providing chat facilities to thousands of users. Each network uses server computers which host a number of chat rooms or channels, often devoted to conversation on a particular theme.

- Microsoft Chat is a client program provided free as a component of Windows 98. Conversations may appear as plain text or in the style of a cartoon strip.

- Chat rooms (or channels) may be hosted by an operator, who can expel users for breaking the agreed rules or "netiquette". Experienced users have their own set of "emoticons" to express feelings and abbreviations to save typing.

- The Whisper Box in Microsoft Chat allows private conversation between a small number of selected users, in contrast to the normal chat which is open to all comers.

- Help for beginners and the names of chat servers may be available from the Web site of your Internet Service Provider.

- Internet Service Providers such as MSN provide chats with celebrities and scheduled chats about subjects of common interest including major sporting events.

9. MICROSOFT FAX

Introduction

Stand-alone facsimile machines have been used for a long time to send an exact copy of a document to another destination, via the telephone network. Nowadays a computer fitted with a voice/fax modem can undertake much of this role, with some limitations.

In order to fax a document from a computer, the document must be running in a Windows application or saved as a file on the hard disc. So a piece of paper which includes a picture will probably need to be scanned into the computer. However, once on the screen it's a simple matter to fax it to another destination. Although there are several ways to send a fax, the basic method is simply to print the document to a fax "printer" - a printer driver which diverts the document to the remote fax machine or fax modem. A fax wizard then guides you through the rest of the process, including the entry of the fax number of the destination fax machine (or modem).

The fax modem, especially the internal variant, saves space on your desktop compared with the more bulky dedicated fax machine, which is also likely to be more expensive. The stand-alone fax machine is certainly less versatile than the modem which has so many additional functions such as e-mail, surfing the Internet and video conferencing.

One drawback is that many modems require the computer to be left switched on with the fax software running in the background, in order to receive faxes. However, the latest *self memory* modems such as the Pace 56 Solo can function with the computer switched off. Also, some computers can be left in "standby" mode, to "wake up" when a fax call is received (discussed later in "**Receiving Faxes**").

In a busy office environment it's clearly an advantage to be able to send a fax direct from an application such as Microsoft Word or Excel. The alternative is to print out the document on paper before taking it to the nearest fax machine and joining the queue of people. While a modem delivers incoming faxes straight to your own hard disc, with the stand-alone fax machine you may be reliant on someone else to distribute the fax sheets.

Faxes received on a dedicated fax machine are automatically printed onto special paper which may be of poor quality. With the computer fax you don't have to print the document at all - simply read the fax on the screen and save it on your hard disc. If you do need a hard copy, the fax can be printed on good quality paper on your normal laser or inkjet printer.

Windows 98 and programs like Microsoft Word allow you to choose from a variety of themed fax templates and to design your own fax cover sheet, perhaps incorporating a suitable logo for your business or organisation.

Fax Software

When you buy a modem with fax capability, you should also receive software to manage the sending and receiving of faxes. However, Windows 98 provides its own fax program, Microsoft Fax, although it's not immediately obvious since it's buried quite deep in the Windows 98 CD. Microsoft Fax and the e-mail program Microsoft Exchange are components of Windows Messaging which came with Windows 95. The next section covers the installation and use of Microsoft Fax since it's freely available to all Windows 98 users. However, most of the basic methods also apply to fax software in general.

Some of the features offered by a popular third party fax package (SuperVoice) are also described.

Installing Microsoft Fax

Microsoft Fax can't be installed by the normal method for adding Windows 98 components (i.e. by using the **Windows Setup** tab in **Add/Remove Programs** in the **Control Panel**). Instead you have to use some installation files which reside on the Windows 98 CD in the folder:

D:\tools\oldwin95\message\intl

To install Microsoft Fax, insert your Windows 98 CD in the drive and use the Windows Explorer to open the **message\intl** folder:

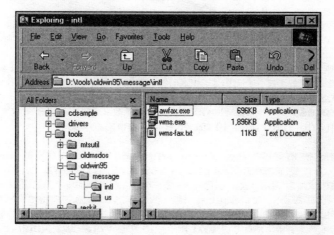

First double click on **wms.exe** to install Windows Messaging (which includes the earlier e-mail program Microsoft Exchange).

Now return to Explorer and double click on **awfax.exe**. This installs Microsoft Fax.

You should now see the **Inbox** icon on the Windows 98 desktop. When the setup is complete the Inbox icon is used to start Windows Messaging.

After installation you should also have a **Mail** icon and a **Microsoft Mail Postoffice** icon on the **Control Panel** as shown below.

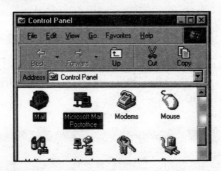

Before using Microsoft Fax for the first time you need to set up a *profile* after clicking on the **Inbox** icon on the desktop. A setup wizard will guide you through this process but you will need to enter a location, i.e. folder on your hard disc, to receive incoming faxes.

There is also a text file **wms-fax.txt** located in the folder **D:\tools\oldwin95\message\intl** shown on the previous page. The text file contains additional information on setting up Windows Messaging and Microsoft Fax. Double clicking on the file name **wms-fax.txt** will load the text file into the Windows Notepad. From here you can read the file on screen or print it on paper.

Once set up, the Inbox can be used to access Windows Messaging (including Microsoft Fax), but as discussed shortly, there are many other ways to access the fax facility. These include sending faxes from Windows Explorer and directly from Windows 98 applications.

Sending Faxes with Microsoft Fax

This section is based on Microsoft Fax, although many of the methods apply equally to other fax software. When you install a fax program such as Microsoft Fax, a fax printer driver is installed alongside of the normal printers. These are shown below in the **Printers** folder, accessed off **Start**, **Settings** and **Printers**.

When sending a fax, the local printer is replaced by selecting the fax "printer" which directs the message to the remote fax machine (or computer and modem).

Composing a New Fax

Microsoft Fax can be invoked from **Start**, **Programs**, **Accessories** and **Fax**.

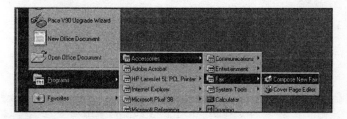

Selecting **Compose New Fax** leads straight into a wizard which guides you through the process of creating and sending a fax.

First you must enter the details of the fax recipient:

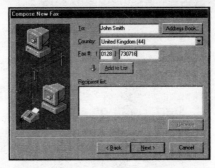

You can also compile an address book and then use it to add to the list of recipients by clicking on the **Address Book..** button as shown above. To create an address book in Windows Messaging select **Tools**, **Address Book** then **Files** and **New Entry**. Then you can enter the fax details for each of your contacts:

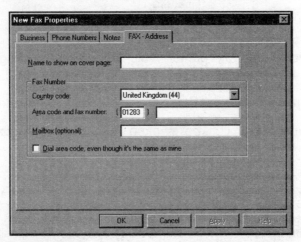

Having entered the details of the recipient(s) or retrieved them from an address book, you are ready to proceed with the fax wizard by clicking **Next**.

You are given the opportunity to include a fax cover page and to choose from a range of styles.

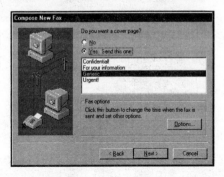

Then you enter the text of the fax, with an option for the text to start on the fax cover page.

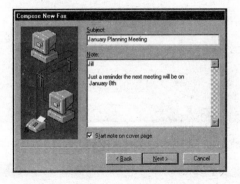

Adding a File

Once you've entered the text for the fax you can choose to *append* a file. This will be sent as an additional fax sheet(s) after your cover sheet and any notes you have entered. Clicking **Add File...** allows you to select the required document from your hard disc.

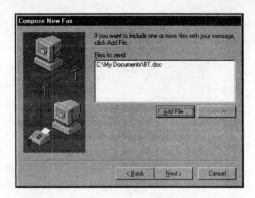

After clicking **Next** you are told that the fax is ready to send. Clicking **Finish** starts the process of dialling up the remote fax machine (either a dedicated fax machine or a computer and modem with fax software up and running). A window appears which informs you of progress:

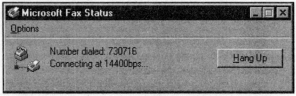

Also shown is the result of the fax transmission.

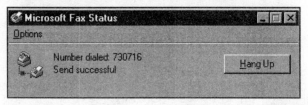

Faxing a Document from a Windows Application

One of the easiest ways to send a fax is from a Windows application such as Word or Excel. With the document to be faxed already displayed on the screen, simply select **Print....** from the **File** menu.

136

However, instead of printing the document to your normal printer (laser, inkjet or whatever), you select a fax "printer".

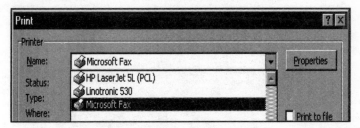

After clicking **OK** to print, the **Compose New Fax** wizard starts up automatically. The method for composing and sending a fax is the same as before.

Faxing from the Windows Explorer

This method is very convenient if you have a document to be faxed which is already saved on your hard disc. Suppose you want to fax a Word or Excel document to a colleague. Simply highlight the file in the Windows Explorer then select **File**, **Send To** and **Fax Recipient**.

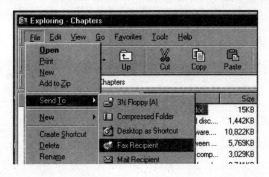

The fax wizard is invoked as before, allowing you to select a cover page, enter the text and send the appropriate document file to a fax destination.

Faxing from Windows Messaging

Start Windows Messaging by double clicking on the **Inbox** icon on the desktop or by selecting **Start**, **Programs**, **Windows Messaging**. From the **Inbox - Windows Messaging** window select **Compose**, **New Fax**.

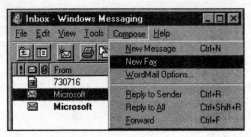

This starts the **Compose New Fax** wizard described previously.

Microsoft Word Fax Wizard

The previous methods of sending a fax all lead to the same Windows fax wizard. Microsoft Word has its own fax wizard accessible through **File** and **New** and **Letters and Faxes**.

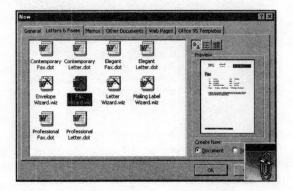

Selecting this fax wizard allows you to use various templates for different styles of fax cover sheet. You can also start the Word 97 fax wizard using **File**, **Send To** and **Fax Recipient**.

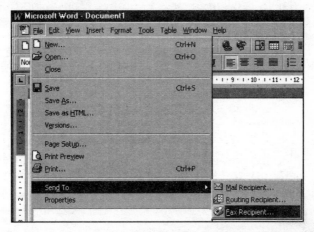

In Microsoft Word 97, the fax wizard allows you to choose which fax program (already installed on your computer) to use. Apart from Microsoft Fax, these might include, for example, WinFax Pro or SuperVoice. There is also a choice of fax cover sheets and a facility for compiling your own address book.

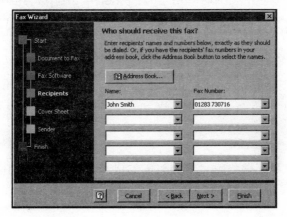

Receiving Faxes with Microsoft Fax

In order to receive faxes, Windows Messaging needs to be up and running with the modem switched on. If you are using the computer for other work you will probably have Windows Messaging minimised on the Windows Taskbar. This will also show a small icon on the extreme right representing a fax machine:

When you wish to receive a fax, click on the fax machine icon on the Taskbar. Then click **Answer Now** on the **Microsoft Fax Status** window which appears.

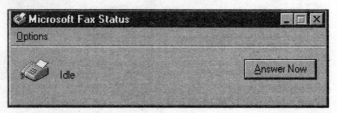

Microsoft Fax will now make the connection with the other fax machine and then receive the pages of the fax. You will be informed as each page is successfully transmitted and when the whole process is finished.

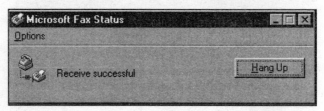

Incoming fax messages are placed in the Windows Messaging Inbox as shown on the next page.

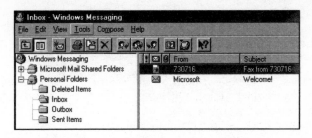

As can be seen from the above Inbox, the fax from 730716 is stored alongside of an e-mail message. This is because Microsoft Messaging is a complete mail service also containing the e-mail program Microsoft Exchange - a predecessor to Outlook Express which is discussed elsewhere in this book.

To view the contents of a fax, double click on its row in the Inbox. The contents of the fax will be displayed in the window **Imaging - Image Document in Windows Messaging**.

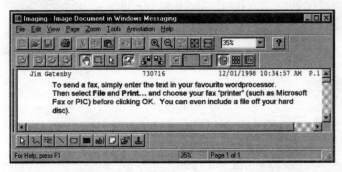

The Inbox provides a full range of tools for managing faxes, accessed off the **File** menu. These include options to **Copy**, **Move**, **Delete** and **Print** faxes. When new faxes are received they are automatically saved in the Inbox, but you can also save them in a directory of your choice using **Save As...**. The **Inbox File** menu for managing messages (fax and e-mail) is shown on the next page.

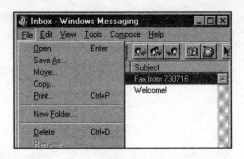

Receiving Faxes when the Computer is Off

A disadvantage with many modem systems is that you can't receive faxes when the computer is switched off. One solution is a self memory modem like the Pace 56 Solo, which can save fax and voice messages by operating as a stand-alone device.

Some computers have *Power Management* facilities which cause the hard disc and monitor to be shut down if not used for a while. In some cases the system can be "woken" by the ringing of a telephone. The fax software needs to be running and the modem switched on before the computer enters the "standby" mode.

You can examine the Power Management capabilities of your computer by selecting **Start**, **Settings** and **Control Panel** and double clicking on the **Power Management** icon. It may also be necessary to alter the Power Management settings in your computer's BIOS. On starting the computer, an instruction should appear on the screen, such as:

"Press Del to enter SETUP"

This should allow you to enter the BIOS and make changes to your machine's configuration. If you now select **POWER MANAGEMENT SETUP** you may be able to set the computer to "wake up" when the telephone rings.

Faxing with SuperVoice

The fax program Microsoft Fax discussed previously, is part of a complete messaging system (including both fax and e-mail facilities), provided free with both Windows 98 and Windows 95. However, when you buy a voice/fax modem, the box should include a software package to handle both voice mail and faxes. Such a package is SuperVoice, which is also discussed elsewhere in this book in the chapter on voice mail. SuperVoice includes comprehensive fax facilities, some of which are briefly described in the next few pages.

Installing SuperVoice is simple - you place the CD in the drive then follow the instructions which automatically appear on the screen. This also installs the fax "printer" called PIC Win 95 Fax Printer. As with other packages, a simple way to send a fax from SuperVoice is to "print" to the fax printer from a Windows 98 application such as Microsoft Word or Excel. With the document to be faxed open in the application e.g. Word, enter the main print window using **File** and **Print...** and select the PIC printer from the drop down list accessible in the **Name:** bar.

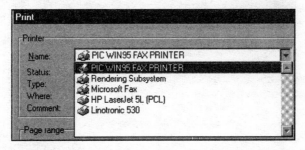

Clicking **OK** causes the SuperVoice software to be invoked. The main SuperVoice **Send Fax** window is shown on the next page.

This window allows you to enter the recipient's details including their fax number, then start the fax process with the **Send** button. However, as shown by the above **Send Fax** window, SuperVoice has many other fax facilities. For example, you can create a **Phone Book** of all your regular contacts and also allocate them into named groups such as members of a club or society.

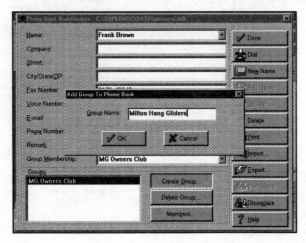

Then you can send one fax automatically to all members of the group using the **Broadcast...** option in **SuperVoice.**

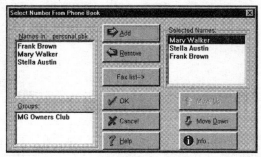

Fax on Demand

This service is widely used to automatically fax information to other people when they fax your number. SuperVoice allows you to store fax images in special Fax On Demand folders. When someone requiring the information faxes you, a voice message will reply with the touch tone digit of the required fax. The caller presses the Receive button on their device and the information is faxed back to them.

SuperVoice provides several other useful facilities such as the ability to attach files to a fax (as discussed in the section on Microsoft Fax.) You can also create your own fax cover sheet with header and footer logos.

Summary: Microsoft Fax

Faxes can be sent and received by a computer equipped with a modem and fax software, offering a neater and more versatile system than the traditional stand-alone fax machine.

- The Windows 98 CD contains the program Microsoft Fax, part of Windows Messaging, which integrates both fax and e-mail systems.

- Documents can be faxed directly from a Windows application such as Microsoft Word, by "printing" to the remote fax machine rather than a local printer.

- Files saved on a hard disc can be faxed using the **Send To** option in Windows Explorer.

- You can create your own fax cover sheets including a personal logo or you can choose from a range of styles using the Windows 98 Fax Wizard.

- Communications packages such as SuperVoice allow the creation of Address Books with the facility to arrange the details of fax contacts into logical groups. A single fax can then be broadcast to a large group of people.

- The Fax on Demand facility in SuperVoice can be set up to allow people to dial into your system and receive, by a return fax, sheets of information which you have compiled and saved as a fax image.

- In many systems, the computer and fax software need to be up and running in order to receive faxes. *Self-memory* modems like the Pace 56 Solo can receive faxes when the computer is switched off. Some computers can "sleep" in a low power *standby* mode then "wake up" again to deal with an incoming fax.

INDEX

Acronyms 116,122
Address Book 23,55
Answerphone 83,94
AOL 9,26-29,34,36
Attachments 58

Cartoons.................116,119,121
Channels 118
Chat 112,115-128
   abbreviations 122
   cartoons 116,119,121
   celebrity.......................127
   channels...............116,118
   nicknames......116,119,127
   rooms......116,118,124,125
   scheduled 127
   servers 115,118,126
   user list.................124,125
   whisper box..................123
COM ports 1,3,4,14-17,22
Control Panel...........................5

Demon Internet...................33,40
Dial-Up Networking 39,41,76
Digital ID............................64,65
Digital signature................64,65

E-mail
   accounts..........38,44,46,88
   addresses 30
   attachments 58-61
   deleting 51
   folders 51,52
   free................................31
   responding 51
   security.......................64,65
   settings..........................38
Emoticons.....................116,122
Encryption 24

Eudora Pro..................29,69-82
   installing 70
   menu bar 78
   new account 72
   trouble shooting............76
   Web-Mail 81

Fax 129-146
   adding a file 135
   address book...............134
   advantages of PC fax.. 130
   computer off 142
   from Windows....... 136-139
   on demand 145
   printer 129,133,143
   receiving 141,142
   sending........................133
   software......................130
Flash Upgrade 2,18
Freeserve..............................28
Full duplex...........................3,88

Groups (e-mail)......................68

Half duplex 3,88
Hotmail...................................31
HTML format.......... 24,43,49,79
Hyperlink, inserting 43,49,50
HyperTerminal 12

IMAP server 23
Inbox Assistant..................53,57
Internet
   Connection Wizard........ 32
   connections 25
   Relay Chat (IRC).........115
   Service Providers 26-33
Interrupt Settings............... 14-17
ISDN 1,20

Login name................................35

Mail servers 23,39,45
Mailboxes 83,95
Microsoft
    Chat 115-128
    Chat, installing 117
    Fax 129-146
    Fax, installing........131,132
    Fax, sending 133
MIME 50
Modem 1
    56K.............................1,2
    applet 8
    choosing............................2
    external 3
    installing 4
    internal 4
    self-memory 129
    testing 10
    troubleshooting 14
    V.90.............................2,18
MSN 9,26-29,35

NetMeeting 99-114
    categories 103,107
    Chat 112
    Directory.......................107
    features 100
    in a call........................110
    installing 101
    making a call 108
    servers 102,106
    session.........................105
    video 110
    whiteboard 111
Newsgroups 66

Online Services 26,32

Outlook Express...........29,43-68
    accounts 45
    installing 44
    stationery.......................62

Pace 56 Solo......................129
Phone Book 36,144
Plug and Play...................5,7,22
POP3 server 23,39,45,72
PureVoice, QUALCOMM..79-81

QuickTime, Apple...................70

Rich Text (HTML)...................49
Rooms.............116,118,124,125

Sharing Applications 113
SMTP server.....................23,39
Sound card...................85,90,97
Speakers...................85,90,97
SuperVoice 84
    faxing.................143-145
    greetings..............92,94,96
    manager 91
    touch tone............93,95,96

Telephone access numbers... 36
Terminal adapter....................21

User name 35

V.90 standard......................2,18
Video camera................104,110
Video conferencing 99-114
Voice files..............................83
Voice mail 83-98

Whiteboard....................100,111
Working offline 48

NOTES

NOTES